Devoted
- AS F*CK -

A Christocentric "Devotional" from
the Mind of an Iconoclastic Asshole

Matthew J. Distefano

All rights reserved. No part of this book may be used or reproduced, stored in a retrieval system, or transmitted in any form or by any means, electronic, mechanical, photocopying, recording, scanning, or otherwise, without written permission from the publisher except in the case of brief quotations embodied in critical articles and reviews. Permission for wider usage of this material can be obtained through Quoir by emailing permission@quoir.com.

Copyright © 2019 by Matthew J. Distefano.

First Edition

Cover design and layout by Rafael Polendo (polendo.net)

ISBN 978-1-938480-46-1

This volume is printed on acid free paper and meets ANSI Z39.48 standards. Printed in the United States of America

Published by Quoir
Orange, California
www.quoir.com

Dedication

This book is dedicated to all my fellow heretics out there who don't give a flying fuck about what the haters have to say.

Acknowledgements

I want to thank my beautiful wife Lyndsay for putting up with my bullshit for all these years. She truly is one of a kind!

And speaking of one of a kind, a huge shout-out to my best friend Michael Machuga, who is one of the most beautiful motherfuckers I know.

To my fellow co-hosts of the Heretic Happy Hour podcast, I must say thank you. Keith, Jamal, and Rafael, could you ever have imagined how fucking awesome this show would end up being? I can't, but then again, I can be quite the self-deprecating bastard (hence the subtitle of this book).

I am also quite thankful for all my personal friends in the Chico, California area: Carlos Sawyer, Erin and Wendy O'Neil, Joel Weaver, Dan and Heather Wysong, Michelle Burdette, Charissa Anderson, Sherie Kermen, and many others. Y'all are the best!

To those who support me on Patreon and in other ways: thank you. Your generosity is inspiring.

And last, but not least, thanks to all the trolls and haters out there. Y'all motherfuckers never cease to amaze me and your words of wisdom always push me to keep releasing iconoclastic books such as this one.

Introduction

Someone once told me that I have a way of saying a lot without using too many words. This got me thinking about how I should one day put together a big book of quotes. Now, a few years later, here I am doing just that.

Simple and succinct quotes can be a powerful artform. Depending on one's worldview or life situation, they can uplift and inspire, or they can offend and upset. As Harvard University Dean of Secondary Schools, César A. Cruz, once aptly noted: "Art should comfort the disturbed and disturb the comfortable." The same rings true for the art of the written word; it will comfort some while disturbing others.

I mention this because some of you reading this book will likely be offended by what I have to say, as well as how I say it. There will be statements made about the religion we call Christianity that will cause your stomach to turn. I will use language that will even force some of you to believe I've sold my soul to the devil himself. And yet, some of you will probably nod your head in approval as if the Lord above sent me as one of his prophets. My take is that I am neither in cahoots with Satan nor a spokesperson for God. Rather, I am just an asshole with an opinion and that y'all can take it or leave it. No harm, no foul.

Honestly, though, I *do* hope that what I have to say uplifts and inspires. And I hope some of my words even cause you to belly-laugh. I believe much of the time, we all take ourselves too goddamn seriously and that what is needed in our lives is a good dose of humor.

So, how should you approach this book? Well, I'd recommend reading one quote per day over the course of a year, but if you want to skip around, that's fine as well. I'm not your fucking parent and have no desire to tell you what to do. But after each daily quote, there *will be* some blank space to journal your thoughts, should you so choose. I'm sure at least a handful of my sayings will cause something to stir inside of you, even if it's just indigestion.

With that being said, please enjoy. Or don't. At the end of the day, none of us should be on this earth to try to appease everyone. I know what I've got to say isn't for everyone, but I also know someone out there will find value here. If that's you, then get ready to put your thinking caps on and have fun with it. Try to get something from the book and may your lives be enriched in some way.

Peace and love and all that good hippie shit.

January 1

In order to live truly free, to live as a human being should, we need to let go of the grudges we hold against all others, even those who oppress us. We need to not return hate with hate, but return hate with love. Both Jesus and the Buddha taught this. In fact, all enlightened masters teach this. It would behoove us to listen so that we can all be set free from the malice that grips our hearts.

January 2

*H*ave compassion on others. You don't know what they're going through. Maybe they've being abused. Maybe they've been abandoned by everyone they once loved. Maybe they just lost a loved one. Or maybe they're just having a shitty day. Regardless, be patient with others because there's a good chance every single person you come across is going through something.

January 3

*F*orgiving others doesn't mean you condone what they've done to you. First and foremost, we forgive others for our own benefit. It gets us out from under the thumb of oppression they've placed on us. Reconciliation comes after they've acknowledged the shit that they've done to you and vowed to never do it again. And I know that doesn't happen in every instance, but at least by forgiving them you allow yourself to be freer than if you didn't.

January 4

We are all God's children. Every single one of us! Don't let anyone convince you otherwise. They are just being shitty by not acknowledging that all of humanity is one family. A fucked-up family, sure, but a family nonetheless.

January 5

I don't know why so many people are afraid of Satan. I mean, if we want to compare the numbers, God kills way more people in the Bible than Satan could ever imagine. In fact, God's kill count is rivaled by no one. If my estimations are correct, it's over 2 million. Satan's? Only like ten. That's nothing. God could take out ten just by farting in the wrong direction.

January 6

Without a doubt, the dumbest thing the church teaches is that the book of Revelation is a play-by-play of what is going to happen thousands of years in the future. How in the actual fuck does that make any sense to anyone? Would it make sense to give a play-by-play of something that is going to happen in 4,019? No? Good. Because neither scenario should.

January 7

A parable can have no "plain meaning." That's not how parables work. They are often, if not always, comparing one thing to another. For instance, many of the kingdom of God parables begin with the phrase "To what shall I compare the kingdom of God to?" which is then followed by a story chock full of allegory, analogy, and metaphor. The point is to get us to think about all the ways in which the kingdom of God is both like and unlike what is being conveyed in the story. To draw a plain meaning from it is to miss the entire point of what a parable is and is not used for.

January 8

The Bible says that the Scriptures are "God-breathed." According to many Christians, this somehow means that they are inerrant and infallible. But you know what else is God-breathed? Human beings. And yet no one in their right mind suggests that humans are inerrant or infallible. Funny, that.

January 9

You can use the Bible to uplift or enslave, bring hope or oppression. Don't be one who does the latter. Don't be a loveless Christian. Be a loving one. Use the "good book" to bring life, not death.

January 10

Jerry Falwell Jr. once said that "a poor person never gave anybody charity, not of any real volume." I guess he never met Jesus, who was among the poorest of the poor. Either that, or Falwell doesn't really give a shit about the "volume" of what Jesus brought. In that case, I guess he wouldn't really be much of a Christian then.

January 11

No one said following Jesus would be easy. Perhaps that's why Christianity has become a religion centered on attending church services, listening to pastors tell us what we already believe, rocking out to shitty music, drinking foamy lattes in the foyer, attending Wednesday night potlucks, and giving money when the basket gets passed around. In other words, it's basically a social club with a few perks, one of which is your fire insurance policy for when you die. No wonder the Church is slowly becoming more and more irrelevant.

January 12

The sooner Christianity sheds its fear-based theology, the better. You reap what you sow, and if you're gonna sow fear, you're gonna reap it as well. But perfect love casts out fear, or so we're told. Which means that if we fear God, we haven't really gotten to know him yet because God is love.

January 13

To say that God the Father is too holy to look upon sin is, to my mind, to say that Jesus Christ is not God. No Christian I know would deny Jesus' divinity outright, so how could they say that God cannot look upon sin when Jesus explicitly did? Is Jesus not the icon of the Father? Is Jesus not God in human form? From the get-go, Jesus stared sin straight in the face and, if we take the gospel accounts seriously, defeated it. So, when it comes to sin, why do we continue to say that the Father is vastly dissimilar to Jesus?

January 14

Jesus said that his kingdom is not of this world. He was right. Our human kingdoms need power over others. Our kingdoms use force as a most trusted tool. Our kingdoms need weapons of war. The kingdom of God, however, has no room for such things. It's a kingdom of love, of humility, of service, of grace, of mercy, and of compassion. It's a kingdom inaugurated by the radical forgiveness of the enemy "other." Indeed, it's an incomprehensible kingdom, inaugurated by an incomprehensible Messiah. But it's a kingdom that is always a reality, should we choose to live in it.

January 15

There are many places in the Bible where the Rapture is discussed. In fact, the Bible is so clear that I'm confounded as to why more Christians don't affirm it. In case you're wondering, here is the laundry-list of reasons we need to believe this clearly-taught biblical doctrine:

January 16

In the Sermon on the Mount, Jesus attaches the anthropological directly to the theological. What I mean by this is that the commands laid out throughout the sermon—love your enemy, bless those who curse you, turn the other cheek, and so on—are given because that's how the Father behaves. Jesus makes this really clear in Matthew 5:48, when he concludes the section with, "Be perfect, therefore, as your heavenly Father is perfect." In other words, God's perfection is seen through his nonviolent orientation toward all people, even those who refuse to follow the peaceful way of the Son.

January 17

When it comes to my Christian faith, I'd rather say "I don't know but I'm going to love anyway" than "Here's how it is, now deal with it." Sadly, many within the faith opt for an attitude that is like the latter rather than the former. For them, it's all about being right, about being certain, about making sure all their doctrinal T's are crossed and their dogmatic I's dotted, instead of perhaps being a bit agnostic but at least loving others and loving them well. Flip that shit around and I'll start finding Christianity a bit more compelling than I do at the moment. I think a whole swath of "nones and dones" will agree with me there.

January 18

When we arrive at the Pearly Gates, I highly doubt we are going to be asked about how many signs we made, or how many events we picketed, or how many Bible verses we can recite, or whether or not we had a Trinitarian theology, or if we affirmed the Nicene Creed or not, or what our denomination was, or even if we were a Christian or something else entirely. If we are going to be asked anything, it's probably going to be whether or not we loved others, whether or not we cared for those around us, and whether or not we showed mercy, grace, and compassion to our enemies and friends alike. So, if there are requirements to get into heaven—and I'm not saying this is how things actually are, just bear with me—I'm guessing it's going to have nothing to do with what one labels themselves, but how one loves regardless of labels.

January 19

Jesus didn't talk about hell more than heaven. To say otherwise is patently false. The numbers have been crunched. It's not even close. When he did talk about hell, though, it was always to warn the so-called religious leaders of his day. They were the ones in danger of hellfire. Let that sink in for a moment.

January 20

"If everyone goes to heaven, what's the point of following Jesus?" some may wonder. But really? That's your stance? Could you imagine only loving your spouse, child, or parent if there were a threat of eternal damnation if you didn't? What a fucking load of bullshit!

January 21

The Gospel is about what God did, not about what we must do. Sure, to know the truth is to experience the benefits of that truth. But not knowing it doesn't change the fundamental truth that God is in the process of accomplishing his promise to reconcile the world unto himself, just as Colossians 1:15–20 says.

January 22

Heaven and hell are experienced now. They are not destinations we go to when we die. They are both now. Either we bring heaven to earth or we bring hell. It's our choice, and it's a choice we make each and every moment, 7 days a week, 365 days a year.

January 23

*L*ove is never embedded in an economy of exchange. Love is free. You can do nothing to earn love, just like you cannot claim to love if you expect something in return. Like grace, it is given away freely, and the more you give it away, the more the world experiences the transformative power of love.

January 24

If Jesus is the only ticket to heaven, what do we do about all the multitudes of people who have never heard his name? And further. What do we do with all the multitudes of people who've been raped by those in the Church who claim to represent him? I mean, I know it makes us feel good to think we're in because we got the password right, but life has got to be much more meaningful than getting the correct code to heaven's gates.

January 25

If God is love—and I believe God is—then all will be well…for everyone and everything that God loves. Which, of course, is everything in existence and everything that transcends existence. That is, existence as such. God would never consign anyone to hell, nor annihilate them, nor allow for them to be consigned to such a place or state simply because love—God—could never tolerate such a thing.

January 26

Stop doing things you think are righteous, holy, and pure because the Bible tells you to. Start doing the right things because they are simply the right things to do. You shouldn't need a book nor the threat of eternal punishment to inform how to behave; you should do what's good for the sake of goodness. Love for love's sake, not because you're scared of what happens if you don't.

January 27

The church is not a building. I don't even think it's solely comprised of Christians. Rather, it's a collection of people who are willing to lay down their arms for the sake of loving their enemies, regardless of their faith tradition or lack thereof.

January 28

People are free to believe whatever they want about Jesus, but if they fail to love others—including their enemies—as themselves, then they are failing to do what Jesus asked of them. After reading the Gospels over and over for decades, I cannot see how you can claim to love Jesus if you refuse to love others in the same exact way you would want to be loved.

January 29

To suggest that "the Bible says" is to make a meaningless statement. The Bible doesn't say anything. Writers of the Bible do. And much of the time, they disagree with one another. For instance, if you were to tell me that James, Peter, and the Jerusalem Church agreed with Paul on all things theological, I'd have to scoff because much of what Paul wrote was in response to their erroneous doctrines. Read the New Testament. That much is fairly clear.

January 30

The problem with Christians is not that they're sinful. The problem is that they act as if their sins are less egregious than the sins of "the world." It's as if they turn a blind eye to the logjam in their eye, and instead only focus on the specks in the eyes of others. For instance, they would likely tell you that smoking pot is evil, but then brag about how much wine they drink, or how much coffee they consume in the morning, or how many Oxycontin tablets they took after their latest surgery (true story). If we want to focus on the sins of others, so be it, but we better make sure we at least have all our shit together first.

January 31

Give me orthopraxy over orthodoxy any day. In other words, give me a non-Christian apostate who practices loving their enemies over a biblically-based Christian who doesn't. I don't want to speak for Jesus, but I think he'd agree with me on that one.

February 1

So many people are clamoring on and on about how violent Jesus is going to be when he returns. This is nothing but people projecting their bullshit onto the divine. At the end of the day, they want a violent Jesus because they are violent themselves. End. Of. Story.

February 2

Universalism is so offensive and scandalous because it strips away our ability to have an "other." If all will one day be reconciled to God, what the hell is the reason to hold a grudge today? If God loves everyone and if everyone is a child of the divine, what justification is there to hold onto your anger and malice? If, at God's table, all will be present and sitting across from you, how can you honestly justify not forgiving them now?

February 3

It always makes me laugh when I hear Christians say things like "Without the Bible, we could never know Christ." I mean, do these folks not realize that people followed Christ before any of the gospel accounts were written down? I guess not, because if they did, they wouldn't say such silly shit.

February 4

Believe it or not, Universalists can still believe in "hell." It's just that they understand that any punishment God may have in store for us actually serves a reconciliatory purpose. Just like when we correct our children for their mistakes, God corrects us for ours. But as any loving parent would rightly acknowledge, parental discipline serves a purpose, namely that it does its job in correcting any and all undesired behavior.

February 5

*L*ife is like a dance, which means that you can't really say there is one meaning to life. Like a dance, the meaning we can draw from it is pretty much infinite. To limit the meaning of a dance down to one thing is to miss all the potential layers of meaning embedded within the dance itself. As any seasoned dancer will tell you, while it may mean one thing to one person, it may also mean something else entirely to another. The same thing goes for life. It's not that life is meaningless; it's that life has infinite meaning.

February 6

If people think you're going to hell, then fuck it, let them. Everyone is going to hell according to someone else. The question is, are you going to let their shitty belief systems dictate what you are doing right now, in this beautiful present moment? Hell no. You're going to go out there and be grateful for every breath you take because this life is too incredible to worry about what others are thinking about you.

February 7

Calling the Bible "the Word of God" is like calling the menu the meal. You wouldn't try to eat the pictures on your menu, so why are you still trying to eat the pages of your Bible? Not only are you going to stay hungry, but you're probably going to get a tummy ache. No wonder Christianity seems so hungry for some actual sustenance, not to mention a little sick to their collective stomachs.

February 8

It fascinates me that those who tend towards a "plain reading of the Scriptures"—literalists, we'll call them—opt not to take Paul's more universalistic passages all that literally. I mean, they are cool with Paul's claim that all are "in Adam" and thus bound for death, but when it comes to being made alive in Christ, all suddenly doesn't really mean all. Or when Paul talks about God having mercy on all, he's not literally talking about all people, he's talking about God having mercy on all those whom God will have mercy on. Given this reading of Paul—and Romans 11, more specifically—it's as if he was the Lead Tautologist at the Department of Redundancy Department.

February 9

At the end of the day, it shouldn't really matter what you believe about God, or Jesus, or the Bible, or any of that. The real question is, do you love or not? Are you compassionate or not? Are you empathetic or not? Fuck the labels. Fuck the metaphysics. Fuck the doctrines and the dogmas. You wanna be like God? Love others. And love them well. Even your enemies. That's the Christian message. Love. Unconditional. Unadulterated. Unbound. Love.

February 10

For Christian Universalists such as myself, the Gospel is far from moot. In fact, without the Gospel—the good news—we probably wouldn't hold to the Universalist position we do. Instead, what we argue is that, while it is far better to know the truth now, that doesn't impact the truth as such. As the writer of 1 Timothy put it: "For to this end we toil and struggle, because we have our hope set on the living God, who is the Savior of all people, especially of those who believe." What I believe this writer is saying is that God is the savior of all people, and it is much better to know that now than not know it now.

February 11

Universal reconciliation and divine justice are not mutually exclusive ideas. The reason so many people assume they are is that justice is often assumed as retributive in nature. Punishment for the sake of punishment. But that doesn't have to be the assumption, nor should it be. Indeed, since God's ways are higher than our ways (Isaiah 55:8–9)—meaning, God's mercy is higher and wider and broader and deeper than ours—that means his justice (reconciliatory) is superior to our justice (retributive).

February 12

How can you love your neighbor as yourself if you think of yourself as nothing but a filthy rag? A used fucking tampon? If you don't love yourself, if you don't have a solid anthropology—one that says you are a beloved child of God, made in God's very image and likeness—can you really love others to the degree that you love yourself? Such a notion seems to make no sense, either theoretically or practically.

February 13

Purity culture makes no sense. Have people even been reading their Bibles? Song of Songs, anyone? That book isn't really about trees, fruits, and flowers. I'm surprised I even have to say this. It's such an erotic book that if you don't get kinda turned on by it, you may need to seek medical help. Either that, or you need to start understanding literary genres a bit better. Regardless, from the looks of things, folks really need to pull their heads out of their asses because no one reading their Bibles honestly could ever conclude that the purity culture is on to something.

February 14

Love is patient. Love is kind.
Love is not envious or boastful or arrogant or rude.
Love is not irritable or resentful.
Love does not rejoice in wrongdoing. Love rejoices in truth.
Love bears all things, believes all things, hopes all things, and endures all things.
Love never ends.
Love does not keep a record of wrongs. Love does not seek vengeance.
Love only works for the good. Love will never forsake you.
Love suffers everything, gives everything, perseveres through everything, and unifies everything.
Love is experienced. Love is tacit.
Love is personal. Love is the reason for existence.
Love is magical.
Love is gazing into your daughter's eyes. Love is kissing her cheek.
Love is tucking her into bed at night. Love is holding her hand when she's scared.
Love is making her laugh. Love is consoling her when she cries.
Love is listening with empathy. Love is not condemning when she's wrong.
Love casts out all fear. Love conquers all death. Love destroys all hate.
Love wins.
Now, read "God" in place of love.

....
....
....
....
....
....
....
....

February 15

Instead of starting our discussion about what it means to be human with Genesis 3, we need to start with Genesis 1. Instead of our anthropology starting with a discussion about the Fall, we need to start by acknowledging that we are, first and foremost, both divine image-bearers and "very good." This is the context of what it means to be truly human. And so, all the passages in the Bible that suggest we are but filthy rags, that we are totally corrupt, that we are "not good," need to be read through the context that we, by extension of whose image we bear, are actually quite good.

February 16

If the Bible teaches us anything, it's that we have three options in how to deal with violence: We can be the violent persecutors of our brothers and sisters (Cain), the persecuted victims who cry out for vengeance (Abel), or the ones who absorb the violence into ourselves and offer forgiveness to all who seek to do us harm (Jesus). Choose wisely.

February 17

You want to preach the Gospel? Feed the poor. You want to follow Jesus? Follow him into the prisons. You want to give your life to Christ? Comfort those who mourn. You want to be the hands and feet of the Lord? Use them to heal those afflicted with disease. In other words, spend more time shutting your mouth and opening your heart. Use your words sparingly and let your actions spread the message of Jesus. Only then will we start seeing the kingdom of God breaking out in the world.

February 18

Grace is a funny thing. It is so universally needed and yet so utterly divisive. On the one hand, if we're honest, we'd all acknowledge that our sin is such that it is only by the grace of God that we're saved. But on the other hand, we don't typically like to think about the "worst of the sinners" receiving such unmerited grace. Perhaps that is why universal reconciliation is so offensive to the more religiously-minded among us. We just can't fathom the worst of the worst receiving such an overabundance of grace. But let us never forget Paul's words in Romans 5:20: "Where sin abounds, grace abounds all the more."

February 19

Job questioned the standard theological formula that says God blesses the righteous while cursing the wicked. His friends didn't. Job was right to do so. His friends were wrong. Be more like Job.

February 20

While the writer of 1 John makes it fairly clear that God is love, full stop, many Christians want to add a "but" after that. This is unfortunate because it often makes God out to be rather two-faced: God is love, but he is also just; God is love, but he is also wrathful. But what if everything we said about God was through the lens that God is love? What if God's justice is an extension of God's love? And what if God's so-called wrath is also an extension of God's love? Well, that's exactly what Universalists like myself argue for.

February 21

Grace doesn't give us license to sin. Rather, it transforms us in such a way that we no longer desire sin. And sure, we all still fall short and miss the mark from time to time. But it is by the grace of God that we realize the error of our ways and at least attempt to do better—to love better, to empathize more, to become more patient and kinder and more merciful. Will we ever be perfect in this regard? Probably not. But grace always seems to light a fire under our ass and gets us moving in the right direction, toward repentance.

February 22

Imagine Jesus sitting down under the Bodhi Tree with the Buddha and a member of the Westboro Baptist Church. Do you really think he's gonna have much to say to the Buddha about hellfire? Fuck no! He's going to be admonishing the Christian bigot, no doubt. That's sort of the point of the Parable of the Sheep and Goats. The sheep are sheep, not because they believe certain "correct" doctrinal statements, but because they have compassion in their hearts. And the goats are goats, not because they're wrong about certain theological claims, but because they refuse to acknowledge the least among us.

February 23

Most often, people who are claiming to talk about God are really just talking about their theology. They've conflated the two because, well, that's just what human beings tend to do. That is why it's always important to hold our theological doctrines loosely, even to the point where we're willing to drop them on the floor. Sometimes shit needs to come crashing down. That's how we let go of the BS and learn to relax into God, or love, or whatever you wanna label it.

February 24

Never forget that the Bible—the book you hold so dear to your heart—includes writings by men who thought the earth was flat, that leviathans swam in the ocean, that gods were tribal and desired virgin sacrifices, that the sun could stand still in the sky, and a bunch of other crazy shit. That shouldn't stop us from studying it or from gleaning truths from it. But it should make us rethink some of the things we've probably been told about what the Bible is and, perhaps more importantly, is not.

February 25

If your religious convictions cause harm to others, then that's a good sign you're not interpreting your faith correctly. Good religion only brings about good fruit: mercy, grace, reconciliation, restoration, compassion, and so on. Bad religion only brings about bad fruit: trauma, fear, pain, suffering, and things like that. Don't get it twisted. You can be religious all you want, just be able to discern the good fruit from the rotten shit.

February 26

There are many reasons to be a Universalist. The biblical argument is sound. The philosophical arguments are solid. But the main reason for me is that it brings healing in the here and now. Think about it: If you believe that, in the end, all will be reconciled and restored, how can you justify holding any grudges today? How can you refuse to forgive those who've wronged you? You can't, really. And that is the biggest reason I continue to affirm universal reconciliation.

February 27

*L*ive your life the way you want and fuck the haters. No matter what, people are gonna hate on you. Have you ever noticed that online trolls are never comprised of people who are actually doing anything meaningful with their lives? You'll never find talented and successful artists hating on others because they're too busy making good shit. Instead, like Jesus said, shake the dust from your feet and keep walking.

February 28

The church I grew up in always looked outside Christianity for the antichrist. What they failed to realize is that a bunch of little antichrists were lurking within its four walls. Any time we act counter to Christ, any time we are greedy, oppressive, unloving, selfish, or hurtful, we are antichrist. So, stop looking "out there" for the antichrist. Look within your own heart and ask if you are acting like Christ or if you are behaving like an antichrist.

March 1

It's sad that when Christians describe God the Father, it sounds less like Jesus from the Bible, and more like Vito Corleone from Mario Puzo's bestseller, The Godfather. Cross him, and you're gonna get whacked. Capisce?

March 2

Some Christians like to point to folks such as Hitler or Pol Pot to prove that not everyone will "get into heaven" when they die. I don't understand this rationale. I mean, it's likely that the folks saying this aren't as bad as Adolf Hitler, but are they really suggesting that their own sin isn't so egregious that somehow, someway, they'll get let off the hook? Are they going to go to Jesus and be like, "Well, Jesus, at least I wasn't as bad as that Nazi bastard over there!" To my mind, if there is grace for our sins, then there is grace for Hitler's. That doesn't mean Hitler won't have a lot of fucking work to do; it just means that God has a lot of fucking time on his hands.

March 3

Seeing God in everyone and everything can be quite an antidote to the chaos that pervades our world. Seeing the spark of the divine in every human heart will only cause you to have more empathy for them, and in turn will cause you to become a more loving and gracious person. Meditate on this and you'll discover just how true it is.

March 4

The first person to witness the Resurrection of Jesus was a woman. The fact that some Christians exclude women from preaching the Gospel, from leading a congregation, from being in a place of leadership within their so-called Church, is not only ironic, but would likely repulse the one who decided to reveal the most important event in history to a woman instead of a man.

March 5

God is not a man. Get over it!

March 6

I don't know if Jesus and Mary Magdalene had a romantic relationship or not. If I had to guess, I'd say no. However, it's fairly obvious Jesus held Mary—all women, really—in high regard. Women in Jesus' day were not viewed highly by their male counterparts, but Jesus had none of that. Instead, he viewed them on equal terms. Mary sat at Jesus' feet, which means she was his pupil. And never forget that she was the first to witness the Resurrection of the Lord. This fact should go a long way in determining just how women are to be viewed by the Church. They are to be co-equals. Anything less is not Christlike. End. Of. Story.

March 7

People need to stop shaming women for exploring their sexuality. Women masturbate. Get over it. They should be masturbating. It's healthy. Plus, might I remind folks that God created the clitoris, and since we men are too stupid—or selfish, really—to figure that thing out, why blame them for taking care of their own damn business?

March 8

One of the worst things about complementarianism is not so much that men believe it, but that they've convinced women to believe it as well.

March 9

If women are really not supposed to be allowed to preach, then why in the actual fuck did Jesus choose a woman to first reveal the Resurrection to? Think about it: Without women, the greatest "Aha!" moment in the history of the world would have never happened. And you still want to shut women out? Fuck outta here with that bullshit!

March 10

The saddest thing about the argument that men are supposed to be the head of the household is not that men believe this, it's that they've convinced women to believe it, too.

March 11

Jesus stood with the "least of these," even going so far as to say that what you do to these folks, you literally do to him. So, if you are against gay people, you're against Jesus. If you're against those locked up in prison, you're against Jesus. If you're against Muslim immigrants, you're against Jesus. Are you seeing the pattern here? The people we often hate and oppress are held, in love, by the very person we claim to follow.

March 12

I often hear the phrase "zealous for God" as if it's actually a good thing. But you know what zeal gets you? It gets you Phinehas, who, because of his zeal for God, rammed a spear through an interracial couple. It gets you Saul, who, because of his zeal for the Law, persecuted followers of Jesus. Zeal is not necessarily a good thing, especially when it's combined with some pretty shitty theology.

March 13

It doesn't really bother me that most Christians don't actually live like Jesus. Hell, I'd be a hypocrite to judge them for their shortcomings, given how often I fuck up. What bothers me, though, is that so many of them don't even bother to try. It's as if they are only playing the Jesus-card so that their precious little afterlife stays secure. But what a cheap understanding of the message and mission of Jesus! What a spiritually baby-ish way to live your life! Jesus is so much more than a fire insurance policy, so much more than an eternal ticket-punching-system. Christians, first and foremost, need to start getting that.

March 14

Being all-inclusive doesn't mean you have to hang out with everyone, or even like everyone for that matter. In all reality, we are only capable of having a handful of close friends. And that's probably a good thing. Relationships take time. Vulnerability takes trust and trust is an ever-growing process that doesn't come all that easily. At the same time, however, we can still treat everyone with respect, still help strangers out when they are in need, and still refuse to create any lines of division that create "in" and "out" groups. That much we all should agree on.

March 15

No one freely chooses to reject God. People reject God, of course. All the time. But no one freely does so. Only an enslaved person would ever reject love. Either an enslavement caused by trauma, by mental health issues, by a chemical imbalance, or simply by not having all the data presented in an intelligible way. Whatever it is, it's something. So, it makes no sense to talk about people freely choosing hell. Only the deranged choose hell over heaven, horror over bliss.

March 16

I wonder what Jesus thinks about all our theologizing. If I had to guess, I think he'd find it kinda ridiculous. Not that he wouldn't find some of it valuable, but I think he'd tell us that we are sort of missing the point much of the time. "Love others. Help the poor. Open your home when tragedy strikes. Confront injustices peacefully." These are the things he'd probably tell us to focus on, not so much the theological mumbo-jumbo we tend to emphasize.

March 17

Fire and brimstone preachers need to slow their fucking roll. God is not Hitler. Nor is God Pol-Pot, Stalin, Mao, or Genghis Khan. Those guys, if given the opportunity, may roast others for all eternity, but God is not an asshole and the afterlife doesn't have a divine Auschwitz or Gulag for all those who didn't pray the magic prayer.

March 18

I would hope that Christians who claim to love others would never allow hell to last forever. I would hope that if given the chance, they'd break down the gates of hell so that those who wanted to leave could. And if people still chose to stay in their wretched state, then Christians would drag their asses out of there and get them some professional help because anyone who would continue to be tormented in objective horror needs help in the most obvious of ways.

March 19

The chasm between heaven and hell is so great that no one can pass from one side to the other. Both the rich man and Lazarus experienced this. Luckily for us, Christ came and did away with that chasm, thus demonstrating God's love for all of us. And given enough time, the Hound of Heaven will seek out all the lost until we live blissfully as one family.

March 20

*P*eace is not simply nonviolence. Peace is a way of living and being in the world. Peace starts in the heart. It starts with resting in the arms of God and knowing you are a beloved child of the divine. And then it works outward into the universe.

March 21

In Isaiah 53:9, the writer tells us that "he [the Suffering Servant] had done no violence." To that end, if we are going to equate Jesus with the Suffering Servant figure, we must conclude that Jesus, too, commits no acts of violence. Indeed, he is the peaceful messiah, rather than the warrior-type many within Christianity say he is.

March 22

If the only difference between the saved and the damned is the choice one makes about Jesus, then how are they not their own savior? Think about it. If, on the one hand, a Christian chooses Jesus in this life and is rewarded with everlasting bliss in heaven, but a non-Christian fails to choose Jesus in this life and is punished with everlasting torment in hell, then the only fundamental difference between the two is what that individual did. That, to my mind, is far too egocentric and individualistic.

March 23

The Bible states that both Scripture and human beings are "god-breathed." How, in the name of everything holy, some Christians then argue for an inerrant Bible and not an inerrant humanity is beyond me. Any intellectually honest person would look at both humanity and the Scriptures they've written and conclude that, while possibly "breathed" by God, are both fallible and capable of error. It's just so damn obvious that you'd have to either be a corrupt asshole or a complete dolt to not get this.

March 24

I once had a Calvinist friend tell me that if he were born in India, he wouldn't be Hindu, but a Reformed Christian. I'm sure the look on my face was priceless, because that is about the dumbest shit I've ever heard. I was thinking, "No, dummy, you'd be Hindu just like the other billion people in your country." But I didn't say anything. People are gonna believe what they want to believe, and if this dude was convinced that God would predestine to save him instead of all the rest of his countrymen, then fuck it, have at it, I say.

March 25

Most of our churches are missing the point about where they need to change. People be like: Stop oppressing the LGBTQ community; stop telling us that we are wretched worms; stop being so goddamn hypocritical. And our churches be like: Let's put a coffee shop in the foyer; let's update the crappy carpet; let's put together a kick-ass rock band with a skinny-jean-wearing front man to lead us in worship. They're so tone-deaf that I can almost see Jesus face-palming from on high.

March 26

There is a sobering truth about who we are as humans and it is this: Victims often become victimizers. Just read the Torah. It's pretty clear. Hebrew slaves flee Egypt, some time goes by and a lot of wandering takes place, and then they start building a temple on the backs of...you guessed it...slaves. Now, that doesn't mean the Hebrew people were particularly bad. In fact, thank God for the Hebrew Scriptures because, whereas other people-groups papered over the truth of the matter, they at least call it how they see it. Humans, whether religious or not, simply cannot help but play the role of both victim and persecutor.

March 27

The Calvinist doctrine of election has to be about the most absurd thing floating around out there. I mean, put the Bible aside for a second and just look at what fruit it has produced. You've basically got a bunch of arrogant, self-righteous pricks who believe God elected them (and not everyone else) for salvation, or a bunch of scared motherfuckers who think God's gonna burn them alive for all eternity simply because they can't be certain they are among the elect. Sick, I tell ya.

March 28

If God really is going to smite his enemies in the end, if he is going to lay waste to all those who reject him, then God really isn't set apart from us, as the scriptures most emphatically say. In fact, if this truly is the case, then he seems exactly like us: vindictive, retributive, and violent. This raises the question: if God is really just like us, who needs him? Honestly, if this really how things shake out, then we might as well just become atheists.

March 29

Many Christians look to the Bible to be their authority in life. This is stupid. Why? Because if they actually read it, they would realize that the Bible isn't self-referential. Rather, the Bible points to Christ as our final authority. Looking to the Bible rather than Christ is like trying to fill up on the menu rather than the meal.

March 30

I've witnessed more Christian pushback against people using the word "fuck" than I've seen against the marginalization of the LGBTQ+ community, the bombing of other countries, and the detaining of immigrant families. This is beyond sad. It really shows you just how irrelevant Christianity has become in the modern age.

March 31

Christianity has a long, storied history of doing a lot of great things. It also has a long, storied history of committing egregious acts like burning people at the stake and slaughtering women whom they thought were witches. Like anything, it's a bit of a mixed bag. So, pardon those of us who aren't really keen on using the term "Christian" to describe ourselves. I mean, it's cool if you self-identify as a Christian; just be cool with those who typically don't.

April 1

You know what the difference is between a member of ISIS who kills in the name of Allah and a member of the Christian church who kills in the name of Jesus? Nothing except for semantics. Fundamentally, they are exactly the same.

April 2

The judgment of the world happened on the cross, when Jesus cried out to God, "Father forgive them; for they do not know what they are doing." What was the Father's response? Forgiveness. How do we know? The gospels tell us, over and over, that Jesus only does the will of the Father. So, if it was Jesus' desire for the Father to forgive all, then you can be damn sure that's exactly what the Father did.

April 3

The purpose of Jesus' death was not to spare us from the wrath of God. It was to liberate us from the neurotic anxiety our future death causes, as well as from continuing in our perpetual scapegoating ways. That's what it means for Jesus to die "for us." He died for our benefit, in order to expose the systems of power that continue to hold us in bondage and to do away with the power death has over us.

April 4

Taking communion has little, if anything, to do with being a Christian. It's about rejecting our propensity toward creating victims. Christians can do this, of course, but so can every other faith tradition. Which means that we can commune with people of different faiths. In fact, I think we should commune with them and always be looking to reach across the aisle in love for our fellow human.

April 5

Sacrificial logic goes like this: We make a sacrifice to appease the wrath of the gods.

Gospel logic goes like this: God becomes the sacrifice to appease our wrath.

April 6

Grace precedes repentance. Forgiveness precedes a change of mind. Never forget that Christ died for the sins of the entire world prior to any of us giving a shit; or, as the Bible puts it, while we were yet sinners.

April 7

If Jesus is simply your ticket into heaven, then you don't understand Jesus. Sorry, but to use Jesus as a fire insurance plan is to miss the entire point of the Gospel.

April 8

What is the Good News? If you ask many a Christian, they'd likely tell you that the Good News is that Christ died to spare us from the wrath of the Father and that if we believe in him, we'll go to heaven when we die. This is dead fucking wrong. Full stop. How do we know? Jesus brought with him the Good News prior to dying. In fact, his first sermon—found in Luke 4—is the announcement that the Day of Jubilee was here, now. Not tomorrow. Now. Not when you die. Today. The Good News for the poor, the imprisoned, the blind, and the oppressed was at-hand, in their very midst.

April 9

The Father never desired for the Son to be sacrificed. He knew it would happen, but that doesn't mean he desired it. We desired it. We always desire it. That's how we keep the peace in our societies. When shit gets out of control, we blame someone else and let all our collective violence fall onto them. In essence, they become our scapegoat, our surrogate. To suggest that this is God's desire is a classic case of projection. I really don't know a better way to put it.

April 10

The cross, according to Christian tradition, is the pinnacle moment of Jesus' life. It is here where Jesus shows us the extent to which God's love will go. He shows us just how willing God is to look upon the worst of our sins, absorb them, and forgive them. From atop the cross, Jesus—God—gets a bird's eye view of the world. What does he do with this view? Luke 23:34 tells us: He offers forgiveness to all those sinful people who put him there. Who, exactly, are these people? Everyone. Everyone is guilty. Everyone is sinful. And everyone is, in spite of this, known by God and offered forgiveness. Their sins are met face to face by God-incarnate and forever erased from the books.

April 11

I'm sorry, but C.S. Lewis was wrong when he said that the gates of hell are locked from the inside. How do I know? Jesus tore the gates right off their fucking hinges, and unless the devil himself put them back up—which he didn't—then whether locked or not, they aren't gonna really function all that well.

April 12

What I find quite ironic is that in spite of the fact that the Scriptures move humanity away from the practice of sacrifice, Christians revert back to a pro-sacrificial stance with some of their most popular atonement theories. I mean, I understand how one could make the claim that God needed Jesus to die in order to appease divine wrath—that's simply how human beings typically think of things—but you'd think that, given the brutality of Jesus' death and the fact that he was quite subversive in his ways, we would pick up on the overall message that God doesn't need blood in order to forgive, in order to show mercy, in order to show grace. God is love and love doesn't need an exchange. Love just is. It requires nothing in return, unlike sacrificial logic.

April 13

When most of us meditate on the power of God, we think in terms of God doing whatever God wants, simply because he's the biggest, baddest being in the universe. But the Christian message is that God is no such thing. Instead, it's the message that God's power is revealed from "below." It's revealed in his suffering—his suffering with and as us—and then in his ability to transform death into life.

April 14

It's sad that because the justice of our world systems is retributive that we believe God's justice follows suit. It's almost as if Jesus never came to show us that God's justice is not like our justice. But if we paid attention, what we would likely notice is that God's ways are not like our ways. This means that God is much more merciful and reconciliatory than we ever thought imaginable. The Bible teaches this. The cross teaches this. And it would behoove us to take notice.

April 15

I find it repulsive that Christians pushback against the pacifism of Jesus simply because there are a handful of passages where Jesus talks about swords, or one instance where he drives out livestock from the Temple with a whip of cords. It's like, have they even read the Sermon on the Mount? I guess not. Or, at least they don't take it all that seriously. And I'm the one who is accused of being a biblical cherry-picker? Get the fuck outta here with that bullshit!

April 16

My Universalism has been described as having my cake and eating it too. Well, no shit, Sherlock! What the fuck else are you supposed to do with cake? Not eat it? What a stupid thing to say. As if people bake cakes and then throw the whole thing away without enjoying any part of it. Sorry, but if you are vehemently against universal reconciliation, you're gonna have to come up with a better slight against it than that.

April 17

Christian authorities love to talk about how Jesus talked about hell more than heaven. Now, forget the fact that they are wrong about this for a second. What they don't love so much is the fact that he only warned those in authority about it. You'll never hear them talking about that. Coincidence? I think not.

April 18

Have you ever wondered why Christian art isn't really art, but kitsch? I have. And I'm convinced it's because Christianity has, by and large, abandoned the real Gospel for a façade. It's no wonder, then, that real art has been replaced by clichés and stereotypes. You see, art should subvert the status quo. It should make those at the top feel uncomfortable. But within Christianity, sadly, it's the other way around. It does nothing more but embrace the status quo, all the while abandoning its true purpose of bringing about needed change.

April 19

Christians love to point out the violence of Mohammed as proof that the Qur'an is evil. They get a little weird and awkward, however, when you point out that in the Old Testament God's kill-count is in the millions. Can anyone say cognitive dissonance?

April 20

No Christian should be for the Drug War. Jesus told us that it's not what we put in our bodies that defiles us, it's what comes out of our mouths that counts. So, how can we justify legislating against what people put in their bodies? It makes no sense.

April 21

Edwards' God enjoys roasting people over a firepit. Driscoll's God is coming back like a UFC fighter. Bickle's God is going to murder millions of non-believers. But fear not, for Jesus' God is nothing like this. Jesus' God is love, and in love we have nothing to fear.

April 22

I haven't calculated the total count, but I know there have been hundreds of rapture predictions, all of which have not come true. And yet, people still buy this shit. God, we are a dumb species sometimes. Dumb and ignorant. This is why solid, Christological theology matters. Without it, we are left to our own devices and it's painfully obvious that they are malfunctioning something fierce.

April 23

If you can't laugh at yourself from time to time, then you really need to. We take ourselves too goddamn serious all too often, and it makes for a miserable experience. Yeah, there are a lot of serious issues we should be wrestling with, but dammit we need to laugh once in a while. It's good for us. It's healthy. It makes the stresses of life more tolerable.

April 24

When some Christians hear of my Universalism for the first time, they act like I never spent twenty-five years of my life believing in eternal conscious torment, or that I haven't had to wrestle with the Scriptures that I was always told proved most people will be lost to the flames of hell. And look, I get that universal reconciliation can be jarring at first, but if your initial response is repulsion, then I think that says more about you than it does the doctrine itself. You should be hopeful, not pissed. Right? Right? Bueller?

April 25

It's perfectly permissible to believe in hell or the annihilation of the wicked. Just at least be honest for a second and admit that if people do go to hell forever, or are zapped out of existence altogether, we as followers of Christ are to still love them. Jesus said to love our enemies. Full stop. He never put a time limit on this. He simply said to love them.

April 26

It sickens me that some of Christianity's most influential theologians—folks like Tertullian and Luther—actually thought that witnessing the damned writhing in hell would bring them joy and thus cause them to give glory to God. If that's not some fucked-up shit, I don't know what is.

April 27

The Bible is a violent book. In fact, in many places, it actually condones and champions violence. Now, this obviously leads some to believe that God is a violent God, while leading yet others to conclude that God doesn't actually exist. My belief is that there is a middle way, one that acknowledges both the violence of the Bible as well as its solution to solving the problem of violence. To my mind, the Bible is chock-full of violence because it carries us from one theological place to another, from the worship of violent, sacrifice-demanding deities to the following of the nonviolent Messiah from Nazareth.

April 28

Make no mistake: All of us are theologically wrong in one form or another. No one has the corner on the Divine. Not even the Christians. Perhaps not especially the Christians. We would all do well to hold our doctrines loosely, not like some, who hold them with clinched fists.

April 29

So many of our Christian doctrines are essentially hopeless. That is, while it is true that folks hold out hope that they will be saved, that they will enter the Pearly Gates when they die, their doctrinal statements paint a much bleaker picture for the remainder of humanity. In fact, it seems that for the great majority of Christians, at least some human beings must perish in the everlasting flames below. Without this, their whole system of thought would crumble like the Tower of Babel for the simple reason that their salvation is predicated upon being saved from hell.

April 30

For many, there can be no Gospel without the threat of everlasting punishment. Take away hell and you take away the Gospel. This is unfortunate because it means that the Gospel cannot stand on its own as the good news it was meant to be. It means that without bad news there can be no good news.

May 1

You know when your finished cocktail has been sitting at the bar for like fifteen minutes, and half the ice has melted? That taste of water with an essence of whatever booze you've been drinking? That's what the Evangelical Gospel is. Watered down bullshit with only a hint of the real thing.

May 2

Christianity…where a despotic emperor (Justinian) is deemed a saint and a pious martyr (Origen) a heretic. You can't make this shit up.

May 3

Christians: Muslims are violent. They need to be condemned.
Also, Christians: How dare you say Jesus was nonviolent!
Me: [Confused]

May 4

If God, the creator and sustainer of all things in existence, is omnipresent, and if eternal conscious torment is a reality for some people, then it's hard not to think that God, too, would be forever in hell. And if God isn't in hell, then God is not the sustainer of all things in creation, which would mean either another god exists, or, even worse, that hell is its own god.

May 5

The thing about sin is that you don't need the threat of punishment to keep you from sinning. Sin is such that the natural consequences of it are enough of a reason to not do it. But even when you do, even when you fuck up in the worst of ways, there is grace for that. As the Apostle Paul said, where sin abounds, grace abounds all the more. So, go ahead and sin if you must, but realize that no matter how sinful you are, you are only cutting off your nose to spite your face, and in the end, it will be only the compelling grace of God that transforms you from sinner to saint.

May 6

Beauty is all around us, and we'll only notice it if we are paying attention. Think about the beauty contained in the finest piece of classical music. Scientifically, it's nothing but various vibrations from various mechanical instruments placed into a particular order at a particular tempo. But experientially, it can bring you to tears and inspire you beyond your wildest imagination, if only you see it as such. Most everything is like this. If we can open our eyes—our spiritual eyes—we will see the beauty of the divine in everything—in the birds, the trees, the bugs, the wind, the ocean…everything.

May 7

Never be afraid to speak your mind. Don't kowtow to someone simply because they are in a place of so-called leadership. Pastors. Clergy. Deacons. They are all fallible human beings and just because they climbed the ladder to the top of "Christian leadership" doesn't mean they have cornered the truth-market. Challenge them. Ask good questions. And never be afraid to put your foot down if you believe something is not quite right.

May 8

The Bible is so clear that Christianity can't even agree on how many books are supposed to be in it. Is it 66 books? Is it 80? Is it 81? It all depends on where you go and who you ask. But everyone you do ask will always be right. Just ask them.

May 9

Fun fact: The Rapture was invented the same year as Mormonism.

May 10

Could you imagine Jesus standing at the foot of someone about to be burned alive for heresy, yelling "Burn him! Burn him!" Yet, that's exactly what many throughout history have done in his name. Makes you wonder how we've managed to fuck it up so badly.

May 11

The Church may not have invented hell, but they sure did use it to their advantage. I mean, how else would they be able to justify burning people alive in the name of a God who they claim is the very essence of love.

May 12

What I wish more people would grasp is that you don't need an eternal ultimatum for Jesus to be worth following. Sadly, it seems that for many Christians, if you take away hell, you take away a part of the Gospel. But shouldn't the Gospel stand on its own? Shouldn't Jesus be worth following regardless of what happens when we die? Unfortunately, the answer for many is "no, not really."

May 13

Many Christians are so offended by Universalism that it's almost as if they want people to roast forever in hell. It's kinda sick, really, and says a lot about their collective (hardened) hearts.

May 14

The biggest mistake most Christians make is believing that sound doctrine is somehow the most important factor in one's faith. It's not. Sound living is. And sure, without sound doctrine perhaps one wouldn't live out of a place of love for their fellow human. But perhaps they would. I personally know a lot of atheists, for example, who are much more loving than some of the Christians I know. And yet, they don't even believe in God. It just goes to show you that the most important thing in life isn't really what you believe about the divine; it's how you emulate the divine, whether you know God by name or not.

May 15

Christians who believe in biblical inerrancy often ask if the Bible isn't inerrant, how do we know what to follow. What they fail to realize is that, even if biblical inerrancy were the best theory of inspiration, we can't escape the personal subjective lens we bring to the text. In other words, even if every jot and tittle of the Bible is correct—which, by the way, given the allegorical and rhetorical nature of many of the stories, is itself open to interpretation—we still have to filter everything through our fallible minds as well as our personal experiences, all which skew and twist the text in some form or another. This is unsettling for many, which is probably why they hide behind something like biblical inerrancy. It gives them a way out, allowing them to not have to think for themselves.

May 16

All the gods we have created are real. Perhaps not real in any metaphysical way, but real in that they fundamentally affect the world simply by our believing in them. That's the power of the human mind. If we truly believe in a god that wants entire people groups wiped out, then we are going to behave accordingly. In fact, we'll probably believe we are the chosen ones who are to bring this about. This is both awe-inspiring and scary as shit because it means all the asshole gods out there have adherents who are ready to go to war at a moment's notice.

May 17

I don't know about you, but when I take my last breath and come face to face with God, I'd rather be reprimanded for thinking he is too loving than for thinking he is a wrathful monster. If God is like the fundamentalists say he is, then at least my conscious will be clear, and at least I could look him square in the eye and say, "Well, sorry, I thought you were a loving father, not a vindictive little shit. My bad. Do with me what you please."

May 18

*P*utting beliefs before direct experience is like putting the cart before the horse. Both are important components in life, of course, but only with the correct order do either function properly.

May 19

God is love, which means that everything we say about God is through the context that God's primary quality, his very essence, is love. This means that God's justice is loving justice; God's wrath is gracious wrath; God's punishments—if we can even use that term—are chastising and always for the benefit of the one being chastised.

May 20

To understand how God is holy, or set apart, we first must understand what the other gods are like. That way, we can specifically see how God is set apart from the gods. To begin, what we should notice is that all the gods throughout the ages have a desire for sacrifice. The logic goes like this: Make an offering and wait for the blessings to flow forth. If that doesn't work, make a bigger and better offering. In other words, use your actions to get the gods to move. But with God, he is the one who makes the offering to us. We are the benefactors of the offering and it is God's actions that change our minds (repent) and get us to move.

May 21

I'm assuming all those loud and obnoxious Christians who drone on and on about how gay people can't be Christians already dealt with the plank in their eyes. No? They still sin? They still fall short? Well I'll be damned! I guess they don't take the Bible all that literally after all. Shocking.

May 22

The only Christian apologetic worth a damn is to love others unconditionally. If you're not doing that, then you should probably just shut the fuck up. Seriously. You're doing way more harm than good.

May 23

*E*phesians 5:1 tells us to be "imitators of God." But many in Christianity say that God punishes those who deny him with eternal conscious torment, which, to my mind, is punishment for the sake of punishment, retribution of the worst kind. What if we imitated God in this? What if we punished our children, for instance, simply for the sake of punishment? That would be horrific. Therefore, either we need to do away with the command to imitate God, or we need a different picture of God's punishments. I opt for the latter, which is why I see God's punishments as corrective in nature, just like any good father would.

May 24

If Christians really wanted to form a nation based on biblical values, wouldn't they be arguing to eliminate any and all debt every seven years? Read your Bible; that's in there. But I don't think Christians realize it.

May 25

Who would Jesus bomb? He showed us in the Garden of Gethsemane. The answer is "no one." Not even the Romans who were about to put him to death in the most gruesome of ways. So, the fact that a so-called Christian nation would drop the most bombs in the history of the world perplexes me, to say the least.

May 26

Christian nation, my ass! When have we ever been a Christian nation? Never. I'm sorry, but if Christian means allowing slavery, fighting the Drug War, and militarily intervening wherever and whenever oil is involved (or when a country wants to go off the US dollar), then consider me post-Christian.

May 27

To hear Christians who have had two, three, even four spouses, talk about how marriage is "between one man and one woman," is about the juiciest irony out there. And look, I love irony. But this kinda shit is ridiculous. I mean, for real, get a grip! Fucking hypocrites.

May 28

The church has a long, storied history of choosing to be biblical over being Christlike. That doesn't mean Christianity has gotten everything wrong from the get-go. It just means we've abandoned mystery for the sake of certainty. In other words, we've turned our back on following the risen Lord and instead have too often clung to the certainty we feel from following a book. And while it's a good book, it in no way should be our final authority. Christ is, which, ironically, is what the good book so clearly says.

May 29

The free will defense for eternal hell is—how should I put this?—utter rubbish. First off, no truly free person would ever choose hell over heaven. That's absurd. Only a deranged person would do this. And second, given that so many of us have mental health issues, brain traumas, genetic disorders, or have been abused by the very Church that claims to follow the God of love, how can we say we are all equally free to make the correct decision about our ultimate fate? To my mind, we can't, which is why we need to start having a more robust discussion about what human freedom really means.

May 30

Isn't it interesting that the South is called "The Bible Belt," and not "The Jesus Belt?" I mean, the Bible is great and all, but you'd think that folks who called themselves "Christian" would be more interested in associating with Jesus rather than the book he's the main character in.

May 31

Notice how many conservative Christians laugh at liberals for being offended at just about everything. Conservatives have even coined a term for them: Snowflakes. Yet, the minute I say "fuck" or "shit," these same folks get so bent out of shape that they immediately need to take a shower, or perform an exorcism on me. Who are the snowflakes now?

June 1

Christianity is a unified body and always has been...just ask the over 40,000 denominations.

June 2

$\mathcal{P}$reaching the Prosperity Gospel is bad enough, but to convince poor people to give you money so that you can line your pockets, all under the guise that you need massive amounts of wealth in order to spread the Gospel to the nations…that's some next-level shit. I no longer believe in hell, but I kinda hope there is one because these motherfuckers need to spend some time there.

June 3

*J*ust imagine, right now someone somewhere is arguing that you—yes, you, the reader—are going to burn in hell for all eternity. Whether you are a Christian or a Muslim, Jew or Hindu, Buddhist or Sikh, doesn't matter. Someone is convinced God is going to roast your ass for a billion years and then follow that up with a billion more. It really makes you wonder just how sick and twisted we human beings can really be.

June 4

There is no such thing as a homosexual lifestyle. What would that mean, anyway? Going to the movies whilst wearing glitter? Shopping for gay-specific groceries? Saying that there is such a thing as a homosexual lifestyle is just more proof that we are all surrounded by a large degree of ignorance.

June 5

No honest person could ever conclude the book of Genesis is actually suggesting that the universe was created in seven literal days. Hell, the sun isn't even created until the fourth day, so how in the fuck could days one, two, and three each be twenty-four-hour periods? We know God couldn't have used a sundial, so did he create the Timex watch on day one? Sometimes I've just gotta shake my head and chuckle to myself.

June 6

Remember that time Jesus said people would know who his followers were by the bigoted signs they made? Yeah, me neither. I guessed I missed that one.

June 7

Ironically, the Bible Belt is the region in the United States that consumes the most porn per capita. It just goes to show you that prohibitions don't really work. And given how judgmental many in the Bible Belt tend to be, it also shows you that Christians can be quite fucking hypocritical.

June 8

People who need to have a straight pride parade are like kids who complain that there is a Mother's or Father's Day and not a Kid's Day. It's like, are you serious? There are 365 days in a year and you aren't happy that 363 are devoted entirely to you? You need those last two? Stop it. Just stop it already.

June 9

The Bible clearly says that God is love. The Bible doesn't clearly say that God is wrath. That's important because, with anything we say about God, there needs to be a context. And the context in the Bible is love. Love is the lens through which we view God. End. Of. Story.

June 10

If you think that the Rapture is "biblical," just remember that it was concocted the same year the modern lawnmower was patented, and only six years before The Alamo took place.

June 11

No matter what, you are loved. You may not always feel it or experience it in every moment, but it's true nonetheless. The God of Love who created the entire cosmos loves you, and is with and for you in all instances. Take comfort in that. I sure do.

June 12

Anyone who knows love knows God. No matter which name you give God, no matter which holy book you read, no matter who your prophets are, to know love is to know God. And even if you don't believe in God, if you know love, you know God. Don't let anyone tell you otherwise. No one can put God in a box because God is already in the box, a part of the box, and in every space outside of the box. Love can be experienced anywhere, at any time, and by anyone.

June 13

All I think about when I see those anti-LGBTQ signs, or when I hear a pastor go off on how sinful gay people are, is how much gay porn these folks are secretly watching. I'm guessing it's a lot. And it's sad, really. Not because they have same-sex attractions, but because they are living a lie, all the while harming so many of their human family.

June 14

We in the church have done a great disservice by placing so much emphasis on what we must do in order to be saved. And sure, Christians still call Jesus their savior, but when it comes down to it, the only difference between the saved and the damned is what the saved did. It's no longer really about Christ. A much healthier, as well as more accurate picture of the situation, is that Christ saved all whom Christ desired to—which is actually all—and that the only difference between the so-called saved and the so-called damned is whether we have knowledge of our inclusion or not. In other words, there are no in-groups and out-groups; there is only being privy to being included or being ignorant of it. Either way, we're all included.

June 15

*J*esus affirmed every jot and tittle of the Scriptures? I don't think so. In his first sermon, when reading from Isaiah 61:1–2, he leaves off the phrase "and the day of vengeance of our God." When John the Baptist sends disciples to ask Jesus if he is the Messiah, he quotes from Isaiah 29 and 35, and leaves off the phrases "for the tyrant shall be no more, and the scoffer shall cease to be; all those alert to do evil shall be cut off" and "here is your God. He will come with vengeance, with terrible recompense." And when he is questioned by the chief priests and scribes, he quotes from Psalm 110, but leaves off "the Lord is at your right hand; he will shatter kings on the day of his wrath. He will execute judgment among the nations, filling them with corpses; he will shatter heads over the wide earth." Now, does all this mean Jesus was a flippant cherry-picker of the Scriptures? No! It just means he was creative and had a very specific, consistently non-vengeful hermeneutical approach.

June 16

To suggest that the Bible is the Word of God, that it is a book penned by the very hand of the divine, is to create an idol of the most ironic kind. Not only are you missing the point of the book by doing this, but you risk missing out on experiencing God in the here and now, which is really what the book is all about: How do we relate to God in the midst of our current time and place? God inspired the writers of what we call the Bible, sure, but she also inspires us today.

June 17

To trust in God is to abandon the need for theological deductive certainty. But the ego needs certainty, doesn't it? It needs to be able to cross every T and dot every I, for when it can't, it flounders. So, might I suggest that we put the ego in its proper place? Tell it that when it comes to knowing—true, experiential knowing—it needs to pipe down and not be so hasty in applying labels and concepts to everything. Just trust that God is good and that love endures and that the rest will work itself out in the end.

June 18

Maybe I'm wrong about most of my theological claims. Maybe I'm wrong in how I interpret the Bible. Maybe I'm wrong about this verse and that verse, this book and that book. But I know what love is and if God is love, I trust that all will be well. It might not be all that well right now, but with love, all things are possible. That much I know.

June 19

If your theology isn't centered on divine love, then it's not good theology. If you must qualify God's love with some concept like wrath, justice, or honor, then you don't really get it. And look, I'm willing to admit that God loves justice, but let's not be so hasty to think that justice and love are somehow mutually exclusive terms. They're not. And if you say otherwise, then again, you simply don't get it. God is love. Therefore, everything we say about God is in the context of love.

June 20

Donald J. Trump once equated himself with the "second coming of God." And Evangelicals still support him. Honestly, how? Have their collective brains fallen out? Or, is this whole Christian thing just a joke to them and they are now trolling us? I don't know. Seriously, I grew up believing their shit for twenty-five years. Rapture. Hell. The second coming of Christ (aka Trump). All that shit. And now some motherfucker from New York who lives in a literal gold tower says he's the only dude who can solve the world's problems and they all kowtow to his ass? They are seriously ridiculous!

June 21

*A*in't it funny how the dudes who are the loudest about how much God hates the LGBTQ community are typically the ones caught beating off to gay porn or with a dick in their mouths? God, you've gotta love irony like that!

June 22

No, the Bible doesn't condemn "homosexuality." It condemns coercive same-sex acts. It condemns catamism. But it doesn't condemn a loving, same-sex relationship between consenting adults. To suggest otherwise is to do great violence to the biblical text. But more than that. It causes great violence against our LGBTQ family.

June 23

Homophobic Christian: The fact that gay people can't procreate is proof that God doesn't want them to be in a sexual relationship.
Me: You get blowjobs, don't you?
Homophobic Christian:…

June 24

When people tell me that because gay people can't procreate, it means that they shouldn't be in a romantic, sexual relationship, I hope they're willing that after menopause, they stop having sex. I mean, consistency, right?

June 25

Christians who want to defend the sanctity of marriage by not affirming the LGBTQ community would do well to stop getting divorced at such an alarming rate. Now, that doesn't mean I support their denouncement of our lesbian, gay, bi, trans, and queer family, nor does it mean that folks who've gone through divorce should be shamed; it just means that if people want to condemn others for what they do in life, then they better sweep off their own fucking porches first. If they don't, they'll always end up looking like damn fools, hypocrites of the worst kind.

June 26

I'm not saying this is how it is, but maybe God made gay people to see if those who claim to follow him are actually going to love others as themselves. Again, I repeat, this is not how I see things, but if it turns out to be right, I'd say the Christian church is failing here. Miserably. Day after day, week after week, month after month, year after year, it's one massive failing. And if I could borrow something Christians seem to enjoy saying so much, it'd be this: Repent or perish. No, honestly. Change your minds about this issue or Christianity as we know it will die. On second thought, maybe that's not such a bad thing.

June 27

If your theology cannot be applied to your real-life experiences in healthy and beneficial ways, perhaps your theology is not worth having. For instance, if your theology says that gay people are sinful simply for being gay, then that is always going to prevent you from loving them in the way they deserve to be loved. How do I know? I've been on both sides of the aisle. On the one hand, I grew up being told the typical Christian message, one that says God isn't down with gay stuff. And it was not helpful in any way, shape, or form. But on the other, once I shed this view, I was able to openly embrace my gay brothers and sisters and have heard firsthand that that is what they are longing for, what helps them, and what is, in fact, what love looks like.

June 28

If you want to argue that the Bible condemns homosexuality, fine. But at least be consistent and stop eating bacon-wrapped shrimp or wearing cotton-poly blends. Advocate that adulterers be put to death. Be ready to kill your mouthy kids. And if your brother dies without any children, be ready to impregnate your sister-in-law. Oh, you don't want to do these things? Good. I don't want you to do them either. So please stop cherry-picking the Scriptures in order to condemn gay people. Like, seriously. Just stop.

June 29

The fruit of the Spirit are as follows: love, joy, peace, patience, kindness, goodness, faithfulness, gentleness, and self-control. This is a good litmus test to see if you are living in right relationship with the Triune God. Funny thing is that most of the gay couples I know display these fruits, which, to my mind, is proof that they should not be condemned. In fact, they should be celebrated. Loudly. With rainbow flags. And glitter. Lots and lots of glitter.

June 30

How come the so-called homosexual clobber passages are taken so literally, while the commands to love our enemies are nuanced beyond all recognition? It makes you wonder if people would rather be bigots than actual Jesus followers.

July 1

People can have a straight pride parade as soon as it becomes culturally acceptable to ostracize straight people simply for being straight. Until then, just shut the fuck up about it. Fucking insecure imbeciles!

July 2

You are more than welcome to take the Bible as literally as you want. Just at least admit that, according to a literal reading of Genesis, Adam and Eve only had sons. No daughters. I'm tempted to tease out the implications of that but I feel as if you all are smart enough to figure out where I'm going with this.

July 3

It's sad that in many circles, Christianity has become nothing more than a list of don'ts: Don't fuck before marriage, don't smoke, don't drink (okay, maybe just a little), don't cuss, don't affirm gays and certainly don't be gay yourself, and so on. It's all just so tiring and downright boring. I'd rather live life according to what I want to do: Love others, forgive unconditionally, work toward ending suffering, and so on. It is a much more joyous and liberating way to live and never leaves one bored in life.

July 4

If the Bible were written today, my guess is that Jesus would say something to the effect of, "Those who live by the gun will die by the gun." Interesting, then, that a supposed Christian nation like the United States of America would possess more guns than people.

July 5

"What would Jesus do?" you ask? Well, I'll tell you what he wouldn't do. He wouldn't bomb the shit out of people. He wouldn't lock them up in a cage for smoking a fucking plant. He wouldn't picket funerals. He wouldn't make signs that say "God hates fags." To be perfectly honest, I'm really starting to think that Christians who wear those silly little bracelets don't actually give two shits about what Jesus would do.

July 6

If you think Jesus was violent because of that passage where he tells his disciples to grab two swords, then not only are you grossly misreading things, but your Jesus is a bit of an idiot. Two swords? To take on the Roman army? Fuck outta here with that bullshit. Obviously, something else is going on there. You just probably don't want to admit it, because you need Jesus to be a bad-ass Pride fighter who could beat people up for you. Kinda pathetic, when you think about it.

July 7

We've twisted things up so much in the Church that instead of following Jesus, we've decided to use him as nothing but a fire-insurance policy. Instead of celebrating his life, his message, his mission, we've decided to focus only on his death and how it secures for us a blissful future afterlife. But remember, Jesus asked us to pray for God's kingdom to come to earth. Now. Thy will be done. Now. Not sometime in the future after we die. But now.

July 8

God is not a blessing and cursing God. God is a blessing God only. Jesus understood this. That's why he counters Deuteronomy 28 and tells us that God sends rain to even the wicked, rather than dust. Paul understood it, too. That's why he counters Deuteronomy 21 and eliminates the phrase "of God" when talking about the curse that led to Jesus' death. It's not God who sends curses. We are the ones. And both Jesus and Paul took it upon themselves to set that record straight. It would behoove us to listen.

July 9

The Parable of the Good Samaritan is evidence that it doesn't matter if you are a part of the right sect or denomination. What matters is how you treat others. The Samaritans were viewed by the Judeans in the same sort of light as atheists or Muslims are by Evangelical Christians. So, for one of them to be the hero in Jesus' story says a lot. It says that you shouldn't judge others because of what "tribe" they belong to. Instead, you should go about your life always looking for ways to help your fellow human, even if they are on the so-called "other team."

July 10

Calvinism has five essential tenets. To explain them, Calvinists use the acronym T.U.L.I.P., which stands for Total Bullshit, Utter Nonsense, Laughable Blather, Irresponsible Gibberish, and Petty Fuckery.

July 11

If God desires to save everyone, and if God has the power to save everyone, then it's a given that God will. That's how logic works. The question then becomes whether God has the desire and/or the power. I believe God does. You may disagree, and that's your prerogative. But I hope you at least wrestle with what you're saying, because essentially, it's either that God doesn't want to or that God is powerless to do so. And while one or the other—or, worse yet, both—may in fact be true, that's a pill too bitter to swallow for me. It may go down smooth for you, but for me, it induces an overwhelming emetic response.

July 12

Atonement can be broken down like this: At-one-ment. In other words, atonement means to be one with God, to be reconciled to the divine. And while it makes sense to think of things in an economic way—that is, you do X to receive Y—that's not how God rolls. God is not in the business of needing sacrifices in order to bestow blessings upon us. God gives and gives freely, and when we realize this, we can be at one with God. That's the message of the cross, where God would rather become the sacrifice than engage in any violent ritualistic behavior.

July 13

Follow Jesus or don't. It's your call. But please don't call yourself a Christian if you aren't going to at least try to love others as he first loved you.

July 14

We are all scapegoaters. All of us. Christians included. The only difference is that Christians should be the ones who acknowledge it and repent from it. That's the message of the Eucharistic meal, where the altar of sacrifice is exchanged for the communal table and where bodies and blood are exchanged for bread and wine.

July 15

No one said following Jesus would be easy, which is probably why most Christians opt not to follow him. Who wants to actively love their enemies? Who wants to bless those who persecute them? Not many of us. But it's what the Lord asked, so it would behoove us to actually listen.

July 16

Many of us clamor on and on about being more like the early Church. That's fine. It's natural to want to get back to how things used to be. You know, the good ole days. The problem, of course, is that no one today actually wants to lay down their weapons or share all of their possessions. That shit's just way too radical of a notion for our more selfishly-inclined, postmodern Western ways.

July 17

Any Buddhist or atheist or agnostic or Muslim or Hindu or Native American Spiritualist or Sikh or Jew who loves others and shows them compassion, mercy, and grace, is far closer to Jesus than the Christian who has malice in his heart.

July 18

Nothing says "Jesus loves you" like the threat of eternal conscious torment.

July 19

The Greek word for hell is Gehenna. Gehenna is an actual place south of Jerusalem. The average temperature in the summer is 85 degrees Fahrenheit. So, yeah, we shouldn't really be worried about going to hell forever. Seems like if we pack a few pairs of shorts, some tank-tops, and flip-flops, we'll be just fine.

July 20

If you're using the Bible to justify violence against those whom you fear, then you're using it wrong.

July 21

God poured out his anger, vengeance, and wrath onto a broken, bloody, and suffering Jesus so that he wouldn't have to do that to the rest of us? Tell me again how that is not divine child abuse. I'll wait…

July 22

Jesus be like: You can't be called great in the kingdom of God without humbly serving others.

Christians be like: Hold my grape juice.

July 23

You have heard it said, "God hates fags," but I say unto you, "Fuck the idiots who say that shit."

July 24

If the God of the Bible is truly set apart, as Christians most emphatically say he is, then why is he just as sacrificial as all the other gods throughout history? I mean, it makes sense to me that a god like Molech would sacrifice Jesus on an imperial torture device to satiate his wrath, but Jesus' own Father? That shit makes no sense. No fucking sense at all.

July 25

The Bible clearly says that God is love. It never says that God is wrath. One precedes the other, meaning that if God has any wrath, it is in the context that God is love.

July 26

It is rather amazing how offended Christians get over the idea of universal reconciliation. I mean, it's as if they are all in love with Jesus for the sole reason of getting into heaven when they die, while being totally content with the fact that all others are gonna roast. Talk about an adventure in missing the point.

July 27

Pardon my dualism, but Jesus is either the savior of the whole world or he is no savior at all. Either he is Lord over all or Lord over nothing. Either he broke down the gates of Hades or he did not. There are really no two ways about it.

July 28

The Bible can be used to justify just about every atrocity known to man. Slavery? Check. Genocide? Check. The forced marriage of rape victims? Check. Killing mouthy children? Check. So, if you're going to use the Bible as a guidebook for life, make sure you know what the fuck you're getting yourself into.

July 29

Jesus said that his yoke is easy and his burden light. Why Christianity has made everything difficult and heavy is beyond me. I guess that's just human nature—to make things more trying than they have to be. My hope would be that we get back to a place where people find rest within the faith, where burdens can be shed and heavy yokes left at the doorsteps of the church community. Maybe then we'd discover healing on a level not yet seen in human history.

July 30

Cain killed Abel because he believed that Abel had God's favor. Jacob deceived Esau because he desired the eldest's assumed blessing and birthright. Joseph's brothers tried to have him killed because it was believed that one day, they would all serve their younger brother. The take away? We are jealous beings. We always desire what we believe the "other" has. And this desire gets us into a lot of hot water. But Jesus came to help us with this by teaching us that the Father shows no favor to one over the other. God is always with us and for us and showers us all with blessings. Just read the Parable of the Prodigal Son. It's all in there, and it reveals the non-rivalrous heart of God in the most beautiful of ways.

July 31

In the book of Revelation, the writer foresees a time when all tears will be wiped away. To my mind, this can only mean one of two things: Either all of us are going to be reconciled to God in the end or those who are reconciled are going to have a frontal lobotomy so that the lost are forever wiped from our memories. Given the loving nature of God, I'm going to go with the former. The latter seems like a cruel trick, one that I simply can't get on board with. Maybe you can, but I believe the writer had a much more inclusive and universal hope in mind when he penned these words.

August 1

Most Christians probably wouldn't want to admit this, but both Jesus and Paul talk about how everyone will one day pass through "the fire" and that this fire is purposeful and good. In Mark 9, Jesus tells us how this process is what makes us salty, which is a good thing. In 1 Corinthians 3, Paul tells us how all the bullshit we've done in life will be burned away and that we'll be saved, "but only as through fire." So, it seems pretty obvious that hell—if you want to use that term—serves a purpose, which is to purify and restore. It's not about punishing for the sake of punishing, but about undergoing a process of becoming more like Christ.

August 2

No group should have to suffer at the hands of Christians. For instance, even if the conservative Evangelicals are right and that being gay is sinful—I'm not saying they are; just bear with me—what Christianity has done to gay folks is abominable. They've been scapegoated, oppressed, kicked out of homes and churches, and have suffered greatly. So, to my mind, the greater sin is not what gay people are doing, it's what Christians are doing in response to the so-called sins of others.

August 3

"God's ways are higher than our ways" is another way of saying "God is way more merciful than we could ever imagine." Remember, in Romans 11, the Apostle Paul tells us that God will have mercy on all whom God desires, which, unless Paul was speaking out of both sides of his mouth, includes everyone. This often confounds us because we are often less than merciful. In fact, we can be quite retributive. It's simply our "way." But God's ways are not like our ways. God's way is the way of mercy and grace. May we never forget that.

August 4

No one approaches the Bible tabula rasa, that is, with a blank slate. Everyone, including myself of course, approaches the text with presuppositions. Everyone reads the text through the lens of their own culture, theology, philosophy, and phenomenological experiences. And while we can do our best to transport ourselves into the various cultures the Bible comes from—the Bronze Age, Second Temple Judaism, and so on—we can never fully grasp what it would have been like to actually live in these time periods.

August 5

Calvinism: God doesn't love you because if he did, he would save you.
Arminianism: God loves you but he's just a wimp so he can't.
Universalism: God loves you and isn't a wimp, so you're good.

August 6

I find Calvinism so damn laughable. Why? Well, for many reasons, but mainly because most Calvinists live in the United States, which means that God is apparently more inclined to predestine Americans to heaven. If that's not a red flag, I don't know what is. I mean, the Universe is infinite, right? And yet, God is somehow focused primarily on this country of ours that is not even three-hundred years old? C'mon, man!

August 7

Christians love quoting Mark 9:42–50 as a prooftext that some people are going to go to an eternal hell when they die. They would do well to read that passage again. Slowly. Especially verse 49, which clearly states that "everyone will be salted with fire." Yep! You read that right. Everyone. Oh, and let's not forget to mention the following verse which says that this process is good. Not bad. But good…very, very good.

August 8

If Christ's mission was to save everyone—and I wholly believe that was a big part of it—and if some sinners are still lost to the flames of hell for all eternity, then Christ emphatically did not accomplish his mission. And sure, the Calvinists would disagree by limiting the salvific work of the cross; but limiting such an event is—how can I put this eloquently?—fucking stupid. And so, either Christ accomplishes his mission and saves everyone, or he ends up failing in a pretty epic way.

August 9

Jesus is known as the Great Physician, which means he is in the business of healing sick folks. If Christians, then, are to be followers of Christ, we should also be all about healing. So, if the world is in chaos, if it continues to be shrouded in pain and suffering, then that means we haven't yet accomplished our task. We shouldn't blame our patients for remaining sick; we should look internally and ask "What can we do better?" No quality doctor blames his patients for having a disease, so no quality Christian should either.

August 10

One thing I appreciate about the Protestant tradition is their reverence for Scripture. I don't think their hermeneutics are worth a damn, and I certainly don't believe the Bible is inerrant or infallible; but one thing I can say is that they at least value the Bible. Now, if they could only understand that one can still value the Bible and not believe it was dropped out of the sky, then we'd be able to make some headway. That'll be the day!

August 11

Do a thought experiment for me. Imagine your loved ones, all gathered in one place. Now imagine half of them being done away with, either annihilated out of existence or, worse yet, thrown into a fiery place called hell. Then ask yourself: could I ever experience heaven without seeing their faces again? Without holding them tightly? Without caressing their cheeks? Without whispering "I love you" in their ears? Short of a divine lobotomy or something to that effect, I believe you'd be hard-pressed to answer "yes" to any of those questions. That should give us great pause and force us to really think about the implications of our theology.

August 12

Sometimes we need to say no to God. Or, at least, that we need to say no to what our theologies say about God. Not everything we've been told about God is true. That's for certain. God is not a death-dealer. God doesn't cause evil and suffering. God isn't going to punish people for all of eternity. God didn't demand the sacrificial death of Jesus. God doesn't hate gay people. God doesn't think women should be banned from preaching and teaching. God does, however, love everyone; so if it's not loving, it's not of or from God and therefore we need to reject such a depiction of the divine.

August 13

What's striking about the theory of an inerrant Bible is that the Bible itself never makes such a claim. In fact, if we actually read the Bible then we'd notice that it's quite the opposite. From debates about the nature of God to the nature of humanity, to various opinions on what is good, holy, righteous, and true, the Bible takes us on a journey of questioning and wrestling with God. Read it for yourself. It's all there, and we'll only miss it if we place our theories above what the Bible actually says.

August 14

A biblical worldview is not necessarily a Christlike one. On the one hand, a biblical worldview can basically mean whatever one wants it to mean. If a person is a racist bastard, they can probably use the Bible to justify their toxic bullshit. If a person is a misogynist, same thing. But on the other hand, a Christlike worldview should really only come to mean one thing: The universal ethic of love trumps all philosophies, all worldviews, all lenses through which we approach the universe. I don't know about you, but I'd take that view over a biblical one any fucking day of the week.

August 15

There is nothing wrong with praying for others. But if we simply pray and then do nothing, what are we really accomplishing? Probably nothing. What needs to be done is prayer and then action. If we are the hands and feet of God, as the Bible most emphatically says we are, then we need to be the answer to our prayers. Let's stop waiting for a man in the sky named "God" to do something about the injustices of the world; let's take action, with Christ at the lead, and actually get some shit done around here.

August 16

*A*s Christians, we should always err on the side of love. Doctrines and theologies have their place, sure; but if love isn't the lynchpin of our systems of beliefs, then we need to rethink what we hold to be true. To paraphrase something the Apostle Paul once said, without love we are full of shit, nothing more than a clanging cymbal.

August 17

There is no more of a reason to fear a man in the sky named "God" than there is to fear the Flying Spaghetti Monster. Neither exist. If there is a God—and I earnestly believe there is—then the closest word in our language to describe God is "love." And if the Bible teaches us anything about love it is this: there is no fear in love. So, stop fearing a wrathful god because he only exists in our minds.

August 18

No good Trinitarian should argue that God the Father behaves differently than Jesus the Son. Over and over, the Fourth Gospel tells us that Jesus only does the will of the Father, which means that the Father forgives preemptively, that the Father loves unconditionally, and that the Father pursues us eternally. God is the Hound of Heaven and because his will is to reconcile all unto himself, we shouldn't be surprised that all will in fact be saved.

August 19

For many, it's quite blasphemous to suggest that there are things that God can't do. But the fact of the matter is that it's true. God is love, which means that God can't be unloving. God is grace, which means that God can't be ungracious. God is good, which means that God can't cause evil. There are many things God can't do for the sole reason that in him there is no darkness. Rather than being an offense to our theological sensibilities, this should actually give us comfort because it means that God is bound by his love for the whole of creation and for every human being in it.

August 20

It's interesting that with so many atrocities happening daily, Christians focus so much of their collective energy on the salty language some use in their day to day lives. Children are fucking starving to death and folks are upset I said "fuck." American bombs are being fucking dropped on families and folks be like, "Do you have to use such objectionable language?" Yes. Yes, I fucking do. Because sometimes it takes a little salt to wake people up out of their fucking little pews.

August 21

Remember that Bible verse that says "And you will know them by their judgmentalism?" No? Me neither! But I do remember the verse that says "By this everyone will know that you are my disciples, if you have love for one another." Let us remember that every time we claim to follow Jesus.

August 22

The phrase "the Bible clearly says" is an offense to the way in which Jesus taught. Why? Because Jesus spoke primarily in parables, the meaning we draw from his teachings can never be reduced to some "clear meaning." In fact, given the nature of a parable, the meaning we draw from them is like peeling an onion—the more you peel back the layers, the more depth of meaning you discover. To reduce Jesus' teachings down to some "plain meaning" is to miss the point entirely.

August 23

Teaching a Gospel of grace does not mean one doesn't have to repent (change one's thinking) in order to experience the fullness of that grace. If anything, grace is that which causes repentance. In other words, grace is such that anyone who truly understands it cannot help but be moved to change their ways of thinking. So many Christians get the order mixed up. They'll try to tell you that if you repent, you'll actualize God's grace. But this is a cart before the horse scenario. In all reality, grace comes before repentance, for without divine grace, we could never really change our mind about who God is and what God is really like.

August 24

Many Christians act as if Universalism is bad news. It's almost as if the profundity of what Christ did for them gets diminished if there isn't an out group destined to the fires of hell. But take comfort, I would want to tell these folks, because Jesus still matters. It's just that he accomplished much more than you could have ever envisioned. Isn't that still good news? In fact, isn't that even better news than what your pastor might have told you? I think it is.

August 25

It is amazing how much pushback there is from Christians over the notion that Jesus was nonviolent. It's as if we will go out of our way to point out how terrible Allah is depicted in the Qur'an, but then argue that God is just as violent because the Bible says so. Can you say cognitive dissonance?

August 26

If the risen Christ told his disciples to forgive others as he himself forgave them, then the only sins that are retained are those which we ourselves retain. In other words, God doesn't retain sins. As the Apostle Paul once said, "love keeps no record of wrongs."

August 27

God is not a monster. Hell is not eternal. Being gay is not a sin. The Bible is not inerrant. Deal with it.

August 28

If a biblical writer takes an already existing story—say, Enuma Elish, for example—and then "edits" it, that's not plagiarism. It's polemical. Learn the difference.

August 29

Christians, I've got an idea for you. How about you stop blaming "the gays" for disastrous weather events and, oh, I don't know, start acknowledging that climate change is real. I know, I know, science is a liberal agenda, but this crap about God punishing us because of what gay people are doing is about the dumbest shit I've ever heard.

August 30

When it comes to the LGBTQ community, sin is rampant...the sin of not accepting them as they are, that is.

August 31

*T*ake a moment to tell the people in your life how much you love and cherish them. Never take a second for granted and be present in the perpetuity of Now. Life can punch you in the gut. Let me rephrase: Life will punch you in the gut. So, do your damnedest to be here, to be present, to not walk through life always thinking about the past or worrying about the future. Neither exist, except in our minds, and often only prevent us from living in the eternal Now.

September 1

If God's will shall be done, then all will be saved. Unless, of course, God's will is to not save all. But what kind of God is that? Maybe some bullshit Calvinistic deity, but not a God who is love.

September 2

What makes the Bible set apart from all the other mythologies is not that it gets everything right, or that it's clean and sanitary; it's that it includes the voices of the oppressed and victimized who cry out to the heavens for justice. This is unique among all other ancient tales. Whereas characters like Oedipus accept that they were in the wrong, many of the victims of the Bible—folks like Job—throw up their hands in defiance and say, "I don't fucking deserve this!"

September 3

In John 20, Jesus tells his followers to forgive others in the same manner he forgave them. That means forgiveness is free and is contingent upon nothing. Remember, these are the same dudes who ghosted on Jesus just a few days prior. And yet, they were still preemptively forgiven by the Lord. Let that shit sink in.

September 4

If you're waiting for Jesus to return so that you can finally live in the kingdom of heaven, you're not really living. The kingdom of heaven is now. It's in our midst. It's within you. It's at-hand. And sure, I suppose that means it transcends our bodily deaths, but why would we wait for death to experience what's openly available to us at this very moment?

September 5

The Apostle Paul once said that every knee will bow and every tongue confess that the nonviolent messiah named Jesus is "Lord." And yet, when Christians come to the passage where this is stated, they interpret it as if Paul was talking about the very violent Caesar—you know, the tyrannical asshole who coerced his defeated enemies to bow down to him. But Jesus ain't like that. Confessions to him will be laden with praise. They will be freely offered by every human who has ever lived.

September 6

I don't mean to sound crass (okay, I do), but I doubt Jesus gives a flying fuck what you believe about him. What he does seem to give a flying fuck about is how you treat the marginalized and oppressed among us. That seems to be the point of Matthew 25, where those who live like Christ aren't even the ones who proclaim Jesus' name. They just do what they do because it's the right thing to do.

September 7

The funny thing about dualism—viewing the world in starkly binary ways—is that to reject dualism is in and of itself dualistic. So, we must suggest that everything, including black and white thinking, belongs in some way: Take a right turn instead of a left one, stop at the red light instead of driving through, turn the light on instead of leaving it off when you get up to go to the bathroom at night, and so on. This black and white thinking shouldn't be how we approach the big ideas of life, but it certainly can be useful in helping us navigate our day to day lives.

September 8

If the god you worship is in any way like the many tyrants throughout history, then that is a good clue that your god isn't really God. God is love. Therefore, love is God. Anything less than or contradictory to that reality is simply false. And if it is true, then we're all fucked. All of us. Even the person who believes in that god, because like all tyrants, he'll turn on you in an instant.

September 9

Jesus never contradicted "the Law." Sure, he contradicted people's interpretation of the Law; he contradicted the legalistic approach to the Law. But he never contradicted it per se. In fact, he summed up the whole of both the Law and the prophets with two commands: love your God and your neighbor as yourself.

September 10

If your approach to the Bible doesn't allow women or non-binary people to preach, teach, or lead a congregation, then you're using the Bible all wrong. Jesus shows us this. Ironic to some, so did Paul. Women sat at the feet of the Lord and Paul described various women as "apostles." To that end, if you want to be "biblical," that's fucking great. Include women! And admit that if you don't, it's not because your Bible tells you not to; rather, it's because you've got a good case of male fragility.

September 11

It's sad that Christians continue to place the Book above standing in solidarity with the marginalized, or what the Book calls "the least of these." Sad, and ironic. Sad because ostracized groups, ones like the LGBTQ community, continue to be beaten down and trodden underfoot, and ironic because if you read the Book, you'd quickly realize that a major point of emphasis made in it, especially when it comes to Jesus—you know, the guy Christians claim to follow—is that placing the Book over loving others is to stand on the wrong side of history, and, if I may be so bold, to stand in solidarity with the antichrist.

September 12

*L*ife is hard. Sometimes you'll suffer. That's why it's important to not be a dick toward others. Even if you think someone is wrong in their beliefs, even if you think they will someday go to hell, at least be kind toward them. You do nothing but add to the suffering of the world by making your stupid fucking signs. Maybe instead, you should bring them a cup of coffee or something. You know, practice some of that Christian compassion once in a while.

September 13

Sometimes there are no explanations as to why bad shit happens in life. Sometimes awful things happen and it's not because God is testing your faith, or trying to get you to listen. It's just the way this universe operates. I don't fully understand why, which is one reason I still don't have much of an answer to the problem of evil or suffering. God is love. I know that much. So, maybe God can't really do much about suffering except to continue to love us in spite of our ridiculous situation we find ourselves in. Perhaps God can do nothing but suffer alongside with us, and perhaps that is enough.

September 14

If God bases our eternal destination on which faith tradition we hold to—whether we are a Christian or not—then that is a telltale sign that he has an ego problem. Only an insecure deity would act like this. God may care about what we believe, but it isn't the ultimate litmus test in terms of deciding our eternal fate. Not unless God suffers from narcissism. And maybe God does, but if God is love—and I believe she is—then that is not the case in the slightest.

September 15

When it comes to the suffering of others, we often have too much to say. Most of the time, there is simply nothing to do but to sit in stillness with those who are experiencing pain. No vapid platitude is going to help the situation. The only thing that really helps is being present with one another, which, incidentally, actually says a lot more than words ever could.

September 16

Not for nothing, but the only people Jesus warned about hell were those who thought their shit didn't stink. In other words, the so-called religious leaders. He never preached hell to the widow, or the poor beggar, or those possessed by the demonic. No. He preached hell to those who sat in positions of power, those who thought they were God's anointed emissaries. That should be quite sobering, especially to any who hold those same positions or who think in those same ways. Hell isn't coming for the people they despise; it's coming for any who do the despising.

September 17

*I*f God is just like the fundamentalists say, then it seems we should all just be nihilists. That God isn't good and no amount of linguistic or ethical gymnastics could ever change that. Think about it: if what they say is true, then what we call good should really be called bad, and what we call bad is likely to be considered divinely good. Language, then, becomes essentially meaningless. Ethics, too. Maybe that's why the fundamentalist world is shrouded in such confusion and delusion. Maybe the universe does have a little bit of ironic karmic energy.

September 18

To love one's neighbor is to love God and to love God is to love one's neighbor. You can't, therefore, on the one hand, claim to love God if you, on the other, refuse to love your neighbor. The two mandates—love God and neighbor—are so intertwined that, like sides of a coin, they cannot be separated from one another. Perhaps that's why Jesus saw himself in the "least of these," and that what we do to the oppressed and marginalized among us, we literally do unto Christ. That's just how humanity works. That's just how the incarnation works. We are so imbued with the divine that we cannot separate either our humanity from God nor God from our humanity.

September 19

If you want to piss off the so-called religious authorities, just preach a message of all-inclusive grace. Trust me, it's the quickest way to have mainline Christianity turn their back on you. But have hope, for if you preach grace, you're preaching the very same message of Jesus and Paul. And if you ask me, those are good dudes to align yourself with.

September 20

Pornhub reports that the Bible belt watches more porn per capita than any other region in the United States. Which tells me that Christians need to sweep off their own fucking porches before worrying about what their neighbor's porches look like. Or, as Jesus put it, "Worry about the plank in your eye, instead of focusing on the speck in your neighbor's."

September 21

One of the beautiful things the Jewish Scriptures teach us is that it is okay to wrestle with God. It's okay to shake our fist at the sky. It's okay to lament when we are in the midst of suffering. At the end of the day, God can handle it because God can handle anything. God doesn't have an ego problem like we do. Our questions. Our concerns. Our annoyances. Our head-shaking. All of it. God can handle whatever is thrown his way.

September 22

Sin and you'll be met with divine grace. Blaspheme the Lord and you will be met with forgiveness. Tell God to "fuck off" and God will still bless you. Nothing we can do changes God's mind about us. But God's response to our perpetual sinning should change our mind about…well…everything. That's the power of divine grace, of divine mercy, of divine love. It has the power to change everything.

September 23

Could you imagine Gandhi coming back from the dead and killing all those who didn't believe in him and his mission? No? Then why in the actual fuck do we think Jesus is going to come back and lay waste to those who don't believe in him? Surely Jesus is more merciful than even someone like Gandhi, right?

September 24

Driscoll's Jesus doesn't exist. Neither does Edwards' God. Both are nothing but manifestations of their fears and insecurities. And look, I get it. I get why we would want our God to be a bad-ass UFC champion or an ISIS-esque torturer of our enemies. But then again, I can be a sick fuck, full of fears and insecurities myself. We all can. But rest assured that God's still a lover, not a fighter. Jesus is still a savior, not a condemner. And nothing we can do can ever put us at eternal odds with either.

September 25

If your theology causes you to create "us vs. them" systems, then it's time to get a better theology. With God, there is no "us" and "them." There is only us. And sure, some may not accept that truth, but accepting truth has no impact on the truth itself. In other words, objective truth is not altered by our subjective experience of it, nor our lack of experiencing it.

September 26

Suggesting that most humans will freely choose objective horror (hell) over objective bliss (heaven) is akin to suggesting that the mentally insane are free from their insanity. No one truly free would ever choose that which doesn't benefit them or their loved ones over that which does. Anyone who does choose horror over bliss, hell over heaven, has to be afflicted in some way and instead of punishment, what they really need is the type of healing only God can provide.

September 27

*L*et's not be cowards and hide behind the supposed "plain reading of the Bible." Let's instead take a step out from that bullshit, like Job did, and put our foot down when we know something's not quite right. Let's hear the voice of God today, and ask "How can we draw meaning from the Bible in a world that looks nothing like it does when it was written?" Let's be a little more like Job and a little less like his friends.

September 28

Frankly, I'm a little fucking sick over seeing those of various faith traditions fight with one another over who is right and who is wrong. I'm sick of people proselytizing and then inflicting violence on one another when they don't convert. We all tend toward describing our own traditions as "the way," completely missing the point that the true Way transcends our cultural and linguistic presuppositions. When Jesus said that he is the way, the truth, and the life, he didn't mean "join Team Jesus or perish." He meant that peace is the Way and the Way is peace. Nonviolence is the Way and the Way is nonviolence. Love is the Way and the Way is love. Mercy is the Way and the Way is mercy. Compassion is the Way and the Way is compassion. And every tradition or lack thereof can live in this manner.

September 29

The Gospel should make us jump for joy, not tremble in fear. Sadly, the Gospel espoused by most Christians does the latter, not the former. It's hell this and wrath that, and instead of being good news, it's become nothing but a fucking nightmare. Accept Jesus or you'll burn! Repent or perish! No wonder people aren't coming to Jesus. The Jesus of the West has far too great a yoke to bear and people aren't having it.

September 30

I always laugh when I drive by churches with signs out front that say "All Are Welcome." It's like, y'all don't really believe all means all, do you? Either that, or you aren't sure what "welcome" really means. Honestly, I'm sometimes tempted to dress in drag, throw a feather boa over my shoulder, sprinkle some glitter in my hair, and test the "all are welcome" theory. But then I realize I have much better things to do with my time.

October 1

If your Christianity cannot embrace the atheist, the Muslim, the Jew, the Sikh, the Buddhist, the gay, the lesbian, the trans, or any others like these, then your Christianity is a waste of time and an offense to who Jesus was as a human. Jesus embraced all. He stood with the historically oppressed and marginalized, so it would behoove us to do the same. Either that or we need to stop calling ourselves "little Christs." Maybe "little shits" would be more apropos.

October 2

Anyone who claims to follow Jesus but still refuses to allow women to teach and preach needs to shut the fuck up. Sorry for my lack of articulation and tact, but that's all I really have to say about that.

October 3

The reason prophets are never welcomed in their hometown is because the role of the prophet is to critique the status quo, to critique those in so-called positions of leadership. To that end, if anyone claims to be a prophet but doesn't critique his or her leadership, then they are a false prophet. We should be leery of any person claiming prophet status, especially if what they are teaching falls right in line with those on the top of the heap.

October 4

Take time to breathe. Life can often be so distracting that we forget to focus on the here and now, and intentional breathing can help us stay grounding in the present. If Buddhism has taught me anything, it's the power of intentional breathing. In through the nose, out through the mouth, always allowing the thoughts that enter to do what they will, and never grasping at them or judging them. This, we can all practice daily. It sounds simple and perhaps a bit cliché, but it will fundamentally change how we experience the beautiful world in which we live.

October 5

With so much emphasis placed on sin, you'd think that Christians actually believe that where grace abounds, sin abounds all the more. But that's not what the Apostle Paul said. He said that where sin abounds, grace abounds all the more. So, let's start focusing not so much on sin, but on the grace that will abound no matter the transgression. Let's focus on Christ.

October 6

I've often thought how absurd it is that the only difference between the saved and the damned is something the supposed "saved" did in order to gain their saved status. Think about it. Listen to most any Christian talk about salvation and they will always come back to something you must do. If you do the right thing, make the right decision, pray the right prayer, and/or live the right sort of life, then you're good. Eternally so. But if you don't do the right thing, don't make the right decision, don't pray the right prayer, and/or don't live the right sort of life, then you're fucked. Eternally fucked in the worst way. Doesn't that seem rather self-centered?

October 7

The ego does not like grace. That's why so many religious folks despise the actual Gospel. For them, it's all about doing something in order to actualize salvation: Give your heart to the Lord (or else), pray the sinner's prayer (or else), repent (or else), and so on. All these ways of thinking are embedded in both our ego and our religious systems. They all require a sacrificial way of seeing. They all require an economy of exchange. That's why so many of our theologies are sacrificial, dualistic, retributive, and, dare I say, anthropological—nothing more than psychological projection of the most overt kind.

October 8

God is love and love keeps no record of wrongs. So, might I ask, who is keeping a list of all the sins that supposedly keep most of us out of heaven? Because it's not God.

October 9

If anyone is forever lost to the fires of hell, then all of us will be there with them. As interconnected beings, what happens to one happens to all. Everyone, even the worst sinners among us—the rapists, the murderers, the tyrants—has a mother. Judas was loved by someone. His name was Jesus. And if Jesus' act of faithfulness was not enough to one day reconcile even Judas to the Father, then what hope is there for any of us? I can't believe that, though. I must believe that what was done in Adam was undone in Jesus, which means that sin doesn't win. Love does.

October 10

People often ask me how I describe God to my daughter without using religious terms. Simple. I start by asking her if she has experienced love, and when she answers "yes," I tell her that that is God. She's nine years old and she gets it, probably because she's never had the old-man-in-the-sky view of God. It's just too bad most adult Christians do have this view of God, which prevents them from actually experiencing God, or love (but I repeat myself).

October 11

The logic of the cross is not what many in the Church have tried to tell you. It's not a sacrificial act that changes God's mind about us. That's the logic of all the gods from pre-antiquity on. Rather, it's a sacrificial act that changes our mind about God, where God is the giver and we are the violence-demanding "gods." Through the cross of Christ, then, the whole mechanism gets flipped on its head like a money-making table in the Temple.

October 12

What's the point of this life? I'm still wrestling with that. But I believe the Buddhists are on to something with their four noble truths: the truth that suffering exists, the truth of the origin of suffering, the truth of the cessation of suffering, and the truth of the path of the cessation of suffering. It's a sobering truth that this life is shrouded in so much suffering, but there is also a great hope that suffering will one day cease to exist. When this will happen none of us can be sure. But it's comforting to know at some point it will in fact happen.

October 13

Many Christians argue for eternal hell as if they are certain they won't find themselves consigned there. Shall I remind them of that passage from Matthew 7? Where Jesus basically tells his listeners that there will be many who did a bunch of shit in his name and yet will find out that the Lord never knew them? Nah, I better not do that. That's fucking cruel.

October 14

*H*ere's a tip: Stop using the book of Revelation as your lens through which you approach the Gospel. Flip that shit around. The Gospel interprets Revelation; it's not interpreted by it.

October 15

If the Gospel isn't good news for everyone, it's not good news for anyone.

October 16

No one "goes to hell" when they die. That's fucking preposterous. We all spend some time in hell during this life in one way or another, so to suggest that some of us will then suffer throughout all of eternity has to be about the most absurd thing I've ever heard, especially given the fact that we Christians claim that God is love. Love would never do that nor would love allow that.

October 17

Take the Bible seriously but please don't always take it literally. It's chock-full of poetry, hyperbole, rhetoric, apocalyptic language, and includes many literary genres that force us to approach things allegorically. Literalism allows for none of that, and only renders one illiterate when it comes to the Bible. Don't be an illiterate literalist. Don't be a dolt.

October 18

How is it that most Christians believe what was done "in Adam" won't be undone "in Christ?" It's almost as if they don't take Paul at his word. It's almost as if they don't take the Bible literally.

October 19

*L*ove never fails. Which means that no one spends eternity in hell. If anyone experiences hell after this life, it will be for their benefit. As Paul once said, everyone will pass through the fire, and while it will burn up all the bullshit we've done in life, it will still be for our ultimate gain.

October 20

To love is to know God. Anyone who loves knows God. Not just the Christians—not even primarily the Christians—but everyone, regardless of religious labels or lack thereof.

October 21

There is nothing wrong with considering the potential future, just like there is nothing wrong with reminiscing about the past. Just be present in both instances. In all reality, all we have is the present moment, so in all that we do, we should be here now. Ruminate about future plans; just be present whilst doing so. And look at old photobooks; just don't be deceived by them. They aren't real in the same way the present moment is real.

October 22

*A*re there things God can't do? Of course. God can't be that which is contrary to God's nature, which is love. In other words, because God is love, God can't be unloving. Too often, we only describe God in grandiose terms—omni this and omni that. But sometimes it's better to start a conversation about God by describing God in negative terms, by saying what God is not like: God is not unloving; God is not vengeful; God is not capricious; God is not un-compassionate; and so on.

October 23

Not for nothing, but when it came to announcing the Resurrection, Jesus chose a woman. Men then took the "we'll take it from here" approach, which is pretty typical, if you ask me. But never forget, Jesus could have visited Peter first. Or his brother James. But no! He picked Mary Magdalene. That says something, especially in a culture where women were not viewed too favorably.

October 24

Conservative Christians tend to make fun of liberals for being snowflakes, for needing a safe space every time they feel offended. What they don't get is that they are just as big of snowflakes, just with different issues. Try kneeling during the national anthem. Or try speaking out against our gun culture. They'll likely be the first to say things like, "If you don't like it here, you can leave." I know they won't see it that way, but it's true: they are just as snowflakey as the most PC liberal is.

October 25

Wanna piss your Evangelical friends off? Just tell them that God loves everyone, wants to save everyone, and will eventually get her way. Not only will they get mad that you dare suggest how loving God is, but they'll get doubly mad that you don't call God a "he." Boy, oh, boy, that gets 'em every time.

October 26

I'm not sure why Calvinists get so upset about my apostasy. I mean, isn't it predestined that I would turn out this way? Who am I to thwart the plans of the most sovereign God? "Take it up with him if it upsets you so much," I tell them.

October 27

I understand the Arminian justification for hell more so than the Calvinist one. I mean, at least God loves people enough to want to save them. It's just that he's impotent. Oh, I know they don't like that, but still, it's true. If God could save them, he would. He just can't. Because our wills are just too damn overpowering for the impotent God of Arminianism.

October 28

Calvinists argue for the doctrine of eternal hell by saying that God doesn't desire to save everyone. Arminians argue for the doctrine of eternal hell by saying that God can't save everyone. Universalists, on the other hand, simply refuse to believe that God isn't love (Calvinism) nor able to accomplish his will (Arminianism) and thus argue that hell isn't eternal, and that God will in fact save everyone because that's precisely what love does.

October 29

*L*oving the lovable is relatively easy. Most everyone does that. The Christian calling, however, is far more difficult; it's the call to love those who declare themselves our enemy. Sadly, we've either forgotten this or decided it's not all that important.

October 30

The Gospel was never meant to be a fire insurance policy or a posthumous reward system. That's cheap. And it's pretty fucking offensive. The message of Jesus is not, first and foremost, about what happens after we die; it's about how we live here and now.

October 31

If anyone goes to hell when they die, it's those who claim to follow Jesus but who reject the least of these. Read Matthew 25:31–46. Slowly, if you have to. Notice: Are both the sheep and the goats not confused by their fate? Indeed, they are! That's because it doesn't matter what label a person assumes. It matters how you treat the Christ that resides in the hungry, the thirsty, the stranger, the naked, the sick, and the imprisoned. That's what matters. That's what's always mattered.

November 1

No one wants to love their enemies. That's why the Scriptures call it a "cross to bear." You see, the cross leads to death. A violent death at that. Guess what, though? The cross also leads to resurrection. Death always leads to life. That is the Gospel message, and it's the only way Christianity can make sense in light of all the violence and death that pervades our world.

November 2

Saying that there is no longer Jew or Greek, slave or free, male or female, is another way to say that there are no longer any dividing lines whatsoever. Full stop. To that end, let's propose to add that there is no longer gay or straight, cis or trans, black or white, conservative or liberal, citizen or refugee. Again, it's not about specific categories; it's about eliminating all dividing lines in order to embrace the diverse oneness that is the body of Christ.

November 3

If we're being honest with ourselves—I mean, truly honest—then we'd likely admit that we don't need a being called "Satan." We are the satan. We are the accusers, the slanderers, the executioners, the death-dealers. Having a being named "Satan" is just another way we refuse to face the reality that we all can be really shitty much of the time.

November 4

A Christian who looks for every excuse to not live out the Sermon on the Mount in their daily lives needs to look for a different label. Leave "Christian" to those who at least attempt to love their enemies and bless those who curse them.

November 5

People love to get all bent out of shape over essentially meaningless peccadillos like cussing or whether or not people fuck out of wedlock, all the while turning a blind eye to the gross injustices of the world like starvation, perpetual war, the destruction of our planet, human trafficking, and other monstrosities. It's sad, really, because even though you might feel better about yourself for denouncing that foul-mouthed Facebook friend of yours for saying "motherfucker" one too many times, you aren't doing any actual good in the world. You're just a virtue-signaling toddler—no offense to all the wonderful toddlers out there—who needs to grow the fuck up. Like, yesterday.

November 6

If love is patient, then God is patient, for God is love. If love is kind, then God is kind, for God is love. If love is not envious or boastful or arrogant or rude, then God is not envious or boastful or arrogant or rude, for God is love. If love does not insist on its own way, then God does not insist on God's own way, for God is love. If love is not irritable or resentful and keeps no record of wrongs, then God is not irritable or resentful and keeps no record of wrongs, for God is love. If love does not rejoice in wrongdoing, but rejoices in the truth, then God does not rejoice in wrongdoing, but rejoices in truth, for God is love. If love bears all things, believes all things, hopes all things, and endures all things, then God bears all things, believes all things, hopes all things, and endures all things, for God is love. If love never ends, then God never ends, for God is love.

November 7

What do Genesis, Exodus, Leviticus, Numbers, Deuteronomy, Joshua, Judges, Ruth, 1 Samuel, 2 Samuel, 1 Kings, 2 Kings, 1 Chronicles, 2 Chronicles, Ezra, Nehemiah, Esther, Job, Psalms, Proverbs, Ecclesiastes, Song of Solomon, Isaiah, Jeremiah, Lamentations, Ezekiel, Daniel, Hosea, Joel, Amos, Obadiah, Jonah, Micah, Nahum, Habakkuk, Zephaniah, Haggai, Zechariah, Malachi, Matthew, Mark, Luke, John, Acts, Romans, 1 Corinthians, 2 Corinthians, Galatians, Ephesians, Philippians, Colossians, 1 Thessalonians, 2 Thessalonians, 1 Timothy, 2 Timothy, Titus, Philemon, Hebrews, James, 1 Peter, 2 Peter, 1 John, 2 John, 3 John, Jude, and Revelation have in common? None of them claim that they are the Word of God.

November 8

The New Testament word for hell is Gehenna, which comes from the Hebrew phrase "the valley of Hinnom." This locale has a long, storied history within Judaism. And not in a good way. It's a place where children were sacrificed to the gods of the Ancient Near East and where the bodies of slaughtered Jews were dumped after their wholesale destruction. The fascinating thing about Gehenna is that humans—only humans—are responsible for the atrocities that happened there. That is to say, humans cause hell. Humans throw people into the abyss, where the smoke perpetually rises and the worm dies not. It's not God who does this. It's we who are to blame for creating such a vile place of destruction and torment.

November 9

If you go onto social media and get into discussions with Christians, you'd likely conclude that the greatest commandment, rather than being to love the lord your God with all your heart, soul, strength, and mind, as well as your neighbor as yourself, is to prove others wrong and mock them when they don't agree with you. It's sad, really, especially given the fact that this tradition is founded upon a man of unadulterated grace, empathy, and compassion. Sad, and emphatically ironic.

November 10

If you want to lose your faith in Christianity, just check out the comments section under any of Rob Bell's YouTube videos. Just make sure you're ready for the inevitable shitstorm. Actually, scratch that. No one should willingly subject themselves to such toxic bullshit. Instead, maybe go for a hike or something. Or pet your dog. Anything but the comments section.

November 11

Saying God loves everyone: Heresy!

Saying God saves everyone: Heresy!

Saying God doesn't condemn gay people: Heresy!

Saying God isn't vengeful: Heresy!

Saying God didn't write the Bible: Heresy!

Saying God became flesh so that he could assuage his own wrath, thus saving those he flippantly elected while damning the rest to eternal torment: Orthodoxy!

#calvinistlogic

November 12

The Bible is not a rulebook for life. It's not a static text with a static interpretation that is meant to guide every jot and tittle of one's life. It's a collection of stories, from countless writers, editors, and redactors, all with differing theological and ethical views that ebb and flow throughout the history of its compilation. And that doesn't mean we should toss out the Bible. Far from it! It just means we need to take a step back and do our best to see the overarching metanarrative that runs through the whole of the text.

November 13

The Parable of the Prodigal Son teaches us many things, but something we typically miss is what it teaches us about the heart of God. After the younger son squanders his entire inheritance, the father doesn't make him grovel at his feet or beg for readmittance into the family; he runs down the lane and immediately throws him an epic party. This is the nature of the Father's grace. It is freely given, at all times and in all places. No favor is earned because it is our birthright as children of the almighty God.

November 14

Just because Jesus only tells one of the thieves on the cross that he'll join him today in Paradise doesn't preclude the possibility that the other thief won't. It may not be today and it may not be tomorrow, but because the mercy of the Lord lasts forever, it certainly seems possible that God will get God's way and reconcile even the wicked thief. If we don't have hope for that, what hope do we have for ourselves?

November 15

The Jesus who comes back with violence and vengeance is not really Jesus but an antichrist. Make no mistake: If Jesus isn't really the same yesterday, today, and forever, then it's not really Jesus. Sorry but the Bible clearly says . . .

November 16

If you want to advocate for a "biblically-based marriage," that's fine. Just know what the hell you are advocating for. In the Bible, there are at least eight different scenarios that fall under the broad umbrella of "biblically-based," and they are: 1) man + woman; 2) man + brother's widow; 3) man + wives + concubines; 4) rapist + victim; 5) man + woman + woman's slave; 6) soldier + prisoner of war; 7) man + women; 8) male slave + female slave. Again, you're free to advocate for this, but do you really want to?

November 17

Not for nothing, but I've never heard of a Universalist burning heretics or apostates at the stake. I'm sure some of them have done pretty heinous things, but I'm guessing not because of theological differences. On the flipside, I'm guessing most every heretic-hunter throughout Christianity's history believed in eternal conscious torment. And the fruit of such a doctrine is pretty fucking evident.

November 18

I'd rather be wrong about theological matters than wrong about what it means, as a human being, to follow Jesus. In other words, give me orthopraxy over orthodoxy any day. Give me an other-oriented ethic of love over so-called correct doctrines. Loving others never harmed anyone. Correct doctrines? Now that's a different fucking story. Just read Christian history.

November 19

No one ever walked away from Christianity because the people were too loving. Hell, most don't even walk away because Christians sin. They walk away because of the hypocrisy. We like to sit on our thrones of piety and act like our shit doesn't stink. But it does. And sometimes it stinks bad. The sooner we admit that, the better. For everyone.

November 20

The Bible clearly states that no one can say "Jesus is Lord," except by the Holy Spirit. It also says that every tongue will confess that Jesus is Lord. You can draw your own eschatological conclusions from that, if you so choose.

November 21

People aren't born with "original sin." Not the Augustinian notion of original sin, anyway. Sure, we're bent toward doing evil at times, but our nature is not inherently evil. As image-bearers of a good God, we are, at our core, good. It's important to remember this, lest we find ourselves viewing our human family as nothing but filthy rags. We are not rags. We are not tampons. We are human. Therefore, we are good.

November 22

Christians should shock the world. Not by attempting to enforce our backward-ass holiness codes or our propensity toward puritanical living, but by our willingness to forgive and to show unadulterated grace and mercy. That's the difference between holiness and purity. Holiness is about drawing near to God. It's about a relationship. Purity is about adhering to a set of rules and dogmas and has little to do with relational living. It's important to distinguish the two.

November 23

Maybe instead of concerning ourselves with what others are doing in their bedrooms, we should concern ourselves with what is going on in ours. Too often, Christians get all bent out of shape about what "they" are doing instead of being contemplative about our own shit. It's almost as if Jesus never talked about planks and specks.

November 24

We as humans are all imitative creatures. We all copy one another. And don't get me wrong, that's not a bad thing. It doesn't mean we are robots or that we can't make choices in life. We can choose to be creative in our imitation of one another. And we can certainly choose our models. We just have to be conscious about these things and make sure we aren't drawn into rivalry with those whom we take on as models. That's why figures like Jesus or the Buddha are so important. They rejected the way of rivalry for the way of other-centered love, the way of grasping for the way of letting go.

November 25

Christians who claim that only they are the children of God are speaking from such a place of privilege, it disgusts me. Oh, how nice it must have been to be born into a Christian home rather than some tribe from the Amazonian jungle or sub-Saharan Africa. What a special person you must be for God to elect you for such blessing. I mean, do these Christians even hear what the hell is coming out of their mouths?

November 26

Your life will include pain. It will include suffering. There is really no getting around that. But take comfort for the God who holds all of creation in the palm of her hands is a co-suffering God. Emmanuel, God with us. And if God is with us, who can be against us? Have faith in God's faithfulness and know that, in the end, all suffering will be nothing but a phantom of times past.

November 27

Saying that there are biblical contradictions is not really saying anything at all. The Bible wasn't written by one person. If it were, then sure, we could say there are contradictions. Lots of them. But it wasn't. It was written by countless people and was edited and redacted countless times. So, naturally, there are going to be disagreements. That's the nature of an ongoing dialogue. Our job, then, isn't to waste our time and point out the disagreements. It's to discern what's what so that we can answer the question we've always been asking: How do I love God and others in the here and now?

November 28

I'm not opposed to people making money. Pastors gotta earn a living, too. But what some of these so-called prosperity Gospel preachers are doing is fucking disgusting. You need a multimillion-dollar jet to "preach the Gospel?" Because there might be demons sitting in coach? Fuck outta here! Just admit you like the money and what stacks of it can buy. Quit hiding behind a broke dude who rode a donkey and walked around barefoot to justify your greed.

November 29

Isn't it odd that the same book some use to denounce the LGBTQ community doesn't denounce slavery outright? I mean, one can certainly argue that the Bible does denounce slavery, but it takes a creative hermeneutic to do so. And I'm fine with that. In fact, I'm more than fine with it. I think we need a creative hermeneutic. But the one used by conservative Evangelicals is anything but creative, and I think too many people have suffered because of their lack of exegetical creativity.

November 30

My heart breaks for a world scourged by violence.
Duped and deceived by the satan inside us.
Accuse! Convict! Point the fingers at "them."
It's us who are just and they are condemned.
Our violence is good; it's righteous and true.
God's on our side and they'll know that soon too.
With power and might we lord over others,
Accusing the prophets of being false brothers.
Woe to those who confuse Christ for religion,
Who speak devilish things about those already forgiven.
Woe to those who demand blood in Christ's name,
Who spit venom and poison, curse others, and blame.
The grace you demand is abundant and infinite,
Yet the grace you give seems rather impotent.
The grace of God is unfathomable and yet,
You contend Love offers an eternal threat.
A gospel with violence is unfounded and false.
It's the opposite of Christ, a religious farce.
The way of the Christ is the way of the cross,
But in knowing the Christ, all else is loss.
The way of Christ is preemptive grace.
Grace in the midst of a spit to the face.
This model of forgiveness is what sets us free,
Free to love all with unbridled mercy.

December 1

Any church that doesn't strive for peace in our lifetime is not a church worth belonging to. If the church is to be anything, it's to be a peacemaker. And sure, it's okay to have our doctrines and our dogmas, but if those get in the way of making peace with others, then they ain't worth shit.

December 2

The Bible doesn't tell us what love means; love tells us what the Bible means. There is no blank-slate approach to the Bible, so we are always going to view it through some sort of lens. That lens needs to be love—true, experienced, awe-inspiring love. Any other approach will always fall short.

December 3

If I could describe God's perfection in one word it would be this: Mercy. The writer of Luke's Gospel drives this point home in chapter 6. It's a very specific type of mercy, too, one so wide and deep that it always includes our enemies. Read the Sermon on the Plain. To be merciful in the same way the Father is merciful is to do good to those who hate you, to bless those who curse you, and to pray for those who abuse you. Anything less is to not be perfect in the same way that God is. End. Of. Story.

December 4

To all those Christians out there judging and condemning others, what don't you fucking get about "do not judge others?" What the fuck don't you understand about "do not condemn?" All I see from the loudest of y'all is judgment and condemnation: You're going to hell! Repent or perish! Jesus is coming, be ready! No bullshit, but y'all motherfuckers are the reason so many people leave the church. It's not because they hate God, it's because you seem to. And that doesn't mean you don't love your God-concepts because it's obvious you do. You just certainly don't seem to give a shit about Love. That much seems pretty clear.

December 5

The concept of eternal conscious torment is not found in the Bible. It's read into it, typically by people who can't seem to get it through their thick fucking skulls that God, being the Hound of Heaven, would never let one of her dear children suffer for all eternity. I'm sorry, but if one of my children were suffering, I'd find a way to stop it. And if God isn't either as loving or as powerful as me, then we aren't really talking about God, now are we?

December 6

Jesus taught us that no good tree bears bad fruit, nor does a bad tree bear good fruit. So, what does that say about doctrines like eternal hell? A lot, I'd say. I mean, ask yourself how many people were burned to death with eternal hell used as a justification? Too many to count, right? And unless you're a sick-ass motherfucker, you'd have to conclude that that is some rotten fruit that needs to end up in the compost pile out back. Or, perhaps even burned up in Gehenna. Either way, to hell with hell, am I right?

December 7

There are literally seven passages in the whole of the Bible that could, on the surface at least, be used to denounce the LGBTQ community. On the flipside, there are hundreds, if not thousands, that talk about justice for the poor, oppressed, and marginalized. Given that reality, you'd think that Christians would be way more vocal about things like social justice than what others are doing with their genitalia. Talk about yet another adventure in missing the point!

December 8

I don't know about you, but I'm sick and damn tired of hearing all the horrible things Christians say about God. They paint a picture of the divine that looks less like love and more like hate, less like grace and more like malice, less like mercy and more like retribution and vengeance. To my heart and mind, this is nothing but psychological projection, a grotesque anthropomorphism that only terrified and insecure human beings are capable of.

December 9

*E*very time a Christian responds to "God is love" with a "but…" I'm just gonna stop them right there and end the conversation. I'd recommend you do the same. There is no "but" after the passage in 1 John that explicitly states "God is love." Not one. No caveats. No qualifications. Nothing. It's "God is love," full stop. Please understand this. It will change everything for you.

December 10

Universal reconciliation is not an eschatological cop-out, as many would have you believe. It's not a doctrine that allows for people to get a free pass in life. Quite the contrary! It's a doctrine that compels those of us who affirm it to freely offer forgiveness and grace to all those who declare themselves our enemy. Think about it. What sense would it make for the Universalist to hold grudges if they truly believe that, in the end, all will be reconciled and redeemed? None, I tell ya! None whatsoever.

December 11

Life is too damn short to worry about what others are doing with their genitals. I mean, seriously. People who have nothing better to do with their time but make bigoted signs and yell at others on social media about all the dangers of "homosexuality" need to grow the fuck up and find a hobby or something. Go learn an instrument. Learn how to paint. Take a ballet class. Something other than wasting everyone's time projecting their bullshit. Like, for real!

December 12

When it comes to salty language, what I constantly try to remind people is that, on the one hand, you can say the most hateful things to others without using any culturally inappropriate words while, on the other, some of the most loving things are chockful of four-letter words. Remember, words aren't magic. They aren't incantational. They don't have objective meaning. Their meaning is derived from our cultural context and can mean many things in many different situations.

December 13

The Gospel is not for you, or for me, or for him, or for her. It's for all of us. It's Good News because it's good news for everyone. And if it's not for everyone, it's not good. It's bad. It's shit. It's worthless. Remember, the Gospel was preached while we were yet sinners. Meaning, the news was good whether we knew about it or accepted it. Let's not be so arrogant to think it's only for us, the Christians, and not, as the New Testament so boldly proclaims, the World.

December 14

Jesus constantly warned people about where violence leads humanity. He knew the truth that those who live by the sword will die by the sword. He understood that any messiah who was going to use violence would lead their people to destruction. He lamented the fact that Jerusalem was going to fall in a mere generation. So, when Christians continually point to the handful of instances where Jesus appears to justify violence—like when he flipped a few tables in the Temple and when he told his disciples to grab some swords—it only makes one thing clear to me: Christians reject the true Jesus of Nazareth. I mean, if Jesus Christ is the Prince of Peace, as Christians would argue he is, then he is nonviolent. I'm sorry, you can't be both peaceful and violent. Things don't work like that.

December 15

Maybe God can't get his way and save all whom he desires to save. Or, maybe God can get his way and decides not to save everyone. But I believe in both instances we aren't really talking about God. Maybe some sort of demiurge who lacks the power and resources to accomplish his will, or, worse yet, a capricious tyrant whose only mission is receiving praise and worship—because God has an enormous ego, obviously—but not a sovereign God of other-oriented, kenotic love like the one I know and love.

December 16

The god who hates fags is a petty tyrant. The god who sends others to hell is a fucking monster. The god who had his son killed so he wouldn't have to kill you is a petulant little brat. The god who needs honor and glory is a narcissist with an enormous ego. But fear not! None of these gods exist in any place other than the hardened hearts of those who create them. The true God loves gays, never had hell enter his mind, would never kill his own kid, and is secure enough to not base his self-worth on whether people fall down and praise his name or not. The true God is perfectly free to love all whom he wants to love. In other words, everyone.

December 17

The earliest Christians spent years learning how to act like a Christian prior to converting. They had to try it out because of how difficult such a life could become. They had to put the Sermon on the Mount and the Didache into practice to see if it would be a good fit. Nowadays, our churches and leaders do nothing more than put on a melodic song and coax folks into coming up to the altar. Honestly, it seems like nothing more than a dog and pony show that keeps pastor's pockets lined and their coffers filled.

December 18

I'm guessing when it's all said and done, a shit ton of angry and bigoted Christians are gonna be quite surprised and taken aback by who gets through the Pearly Gates. Gay folks. Queer folks. Trans folks. Muslims. Atheists. Pagans. Jews. New-Agers. And I'm also guessing they'll go to Jesus and be like, "What's going on here?" and Jesus will be like, "Da fuck?! Who are you again?" That'll be an interesting day. But I'm guessing those Christians will even come around, even if they are the last ones to be reconciled to God.

December 19

What's fascinating about the book of Hebrews is that the writer could have had the preincarnate Christ quote any text he wanted, and yet he picks Psalm 40:6–8, arguably the most anti-sacrificial passage in the whole of the Jewish Bible. It's as if the Father asks the Son, "You got any last words?" to which the Son replies with an anti-sacrificial mic drop.

December 20

Isn't it amazing how Jesus commands us to love God with all our minds, and yet Christians can be about the most ignorant and doltish people on the planet? I mean, some of them still believe that the earth is flat. No, really. Fucking look it up. They are out there in staggering numbers.

December 21

Make no mistake, Jesus never came to start a religion called "Christianity." He came to lead a life that, while devoutly Jewish, transcended all religious labeling. He came to show us a way of living—an ethic of universal love for the other—that both the religious person as well as the atheist could participate in.

December 22

To build walls around others is emphatically antichrist. Any partition you create, Jesus will tear down. Any hell you put others in, Jesus will snatch them out of. Never forget that the gates of Hades were blown off their hinges in the most dramatic way for all time and for all people.

December 23

*D*eath is not the end. Death has never been the end. It's an event, sure. It's real insofar as any event is real. But it is not the end because God is a God of life, of love, of eternal goodness. And God will get what God wants because love wins. Life wins. In the end, life and love will always win.

December 24

If your idea of putting Christ back in Christmas is getting Starbucks to put an image of little baby Jesus on their cups, then you're missing the point. Like. Entirely.

December 25

Put Christ back in Christmas? How about we put Christ back in Christianity? Now that's a novel concept.

December 26

*A*s my favorite Christmas song goes, "his Gospel is peace." Sadly, many Christians will be among the last to understand that there is no violence in the good news of God.

December 27

*L*ove is love. It is not defined by what genitalia one has or doesn't have. It is not conditional upon believing this or affirming that. It is not contingent upon doctrine or dogma. It just is. And when you experience it, you know it, not necessarily intellectually—as if it can be reduced to some set of propositions or deductions—but on a much deeper level. You know it at the core of your being. In your soul. You feel it in your gut and in your heart, and it always blows apart any of the boxes you've previously tried to place it in.

December 28

Jesus never coerced people into doing what he thought was right. He never forced them to believe in him or his way. Instead, he lovingly motivated them. He showed them the errors of their ways and offered a better way of being a human. He compelled them with passionate compassion rather than coercive strong-arming. To that end, if we are going to believe that one day every knee will bow and give praise that Jesus is Lord, it won't be because they were coerced into submission. Rather, it will be because they were compelled by love.

December 29

The truly free person will always choose love over fear, mercy over sacrifice, restoration over retribution, heaven over hell. Any choice that we make that doesn't line up with the will of God is not a free choice but a choice driven by an enslavement of sorts. Given the best information and working faculties, we'll always choose the good, or God, or love, or whatever the hell you want to call it. Every. Fucking. Time.

December 30

If we aren't sure as to whether or not it's sinful to engage in any non-heterosexual sexual acts, the only question we need to ask is this: Does it violate the ethic of other-oriented love? If it does, then fine, call it sin. But if it doesn't, then it's not. But, to be perfectly frank, this question should be asked of any action we as Christians engage in. One's sexuality really has nothing to do with the matter.

December 31

Why do we look to a book for answers to life's questions when all we have to really do is listen to that still small voice that guides our spirit? If Jesus is alive today, if the Holy Spirit still moves and speaks and informs, then we don't necessarily need a book to tell us what to do. The ironic thing about all this is that the book agrees with me. In other words, the Bible is never self-referential. Rather, it points to another, namely the Word of God, the one we call Christ.

For more information about Matthew J. Distefano
or to contact him for speaking engagements,
please visit *www.allsetfree.com*

Many voices. One message.

Quoir is a boutique publishing company
with a single message: Christ is all.
Our books explore both His
cosmic nature and corporate expression.

For more information, please visit
www.quoir.com

www.ingramcontent.com/pod-product-compliance
Lightning Source LLC
Chambersburg PA
CBHW020108240426
43661CB00002B/76

* 9 7 8 1 9 3 8 4 8 0 4 6 1 *